Books by Dave and Neta Jackson

Hero Tales: A Family Treasury of True Stories
From the Lives of Christian Heroes (Volumes 1 & 2)

Trailblazer Books

Abandoned on the Wild Frontier—Peter Cartwright
Attack in the Rye Grass—Marcus & Narcissa Whitman
The Bandit of Ashley Downs—George Müller
The Betrayer's Fortune—Menno Simons
The Chimney Sweep's Ransom—John Wesley
Danger on the Flying Trapeze—Dwight L. Moody
Defeat of the Ghost Riders—Mary McLeod Bethune
Drummer Boy's Battle—Florence Nightingale
Escape from the Slave Traders—David Livingstone
The Fate of the Yellow Woodbee—Nate Saint
Flight of the Fugitives—Gladys Aylward
The Hidden Jewel—Amy Carmichael
Imprisoned in the Golden City—Adoniram & Ann Judson
Kidnapped by River Rats—William & Catherine Booth
Listen for the Whippoorwill—Harriet Tubman
The Queen's Smuggler—William Tyndale
Quest for the Lost Prince—Samuel Morris
The Runaway's Revenge—John Newton
Shanghaied to China—Hudson Taylor
Spy for the Night Riders—Martin Luther
The Thieves of Tyburn Square—Elizabeth Fry
Trial by Poison—Mary Slessor
Traitor In the Tower—John Bunyan
The Warrior's Challenge—David Zeisberger

HERO TALES

VOLUME II

DAVE & NETA JACKSON

BETHANY HOUSE PUBLISHERS

MINNEAPOLIS, MINNESOTA 55438

Hero Tales, Volume 2: A Family Treasury of True Stories From the Lives of Christian Heroes
Copyright © 1997
Dave and Neta Jackson

Cover design by Peter Glöege
Interior illustrations by Toni Auble

Unless otherwise identified, Scripture quotations are from *The Holy Bible, New Century Version.*
Copyright © 1987, 1988, 1991 by Word Publishing, Dallas, Texas 75039. Used by permission.

Scripture quotations identified KJV are from the King James Version of the Bible.

Scripture quotations identified NIV are from the HOLY BIBLE, NEW INTERNATIONAL
VERSION®. Copyright © 1973, 1978, 1984 by International Bible Society. Used by permission of
Zondervan Publishing House. All rights reserved. The "NIV" and "New International Version"
trademarks are registered in the United States Patent and Trademark Office by International Bible
Society. Use of either trademark requires the permission of International Bible Society.

Scripture quotations identified TEV are from the Bible in Today's English Version (*Good News Bible*).
Copyright © American Bible Society 1966, 1971, 1976, 1992.

Published by Bethany House Publishers
A Ministry of Bethany Fellowship, Inc.
11300 Hampshire Avenue South
Minneapolis, Minnesota 55438

Printed in the United States of America.

ISBN 1–55661–712–7 (Volume 1)
ISBN 1–55661–713–5 (Volume 2)

Library of Congress Cataloging-in-Publication Data

Jackson, Dave.
  Hero tales: a family treasury of true stories from the lives of Christian heroes / Dave and Neta
Jackson.
    p. cm.
  Summary: Presents biographies of fifteen missionaries, evangelists, and other Christian heroes
who worked courageously to share the Gospel with others.

  1. Christian biography—Juvenile literature. 2. Missionaries—Biography—Juvenile literature.
[1. Christian biography. 2. Missionaries.] I. Jackson, Neta. II. Title.
BR1704.J33   1996
270'.092'2—dc20
[B]   96–25230
                                                                              CIP
                                                                              AC

For Trevor and Riley—
young heroes in the
making.

CONTENTS ✺

CONTENTS

DIETRICH BONHOEFFER

He Dared to Stand Up to Hitler

Dietrich Bonhoeffer and his twin sister, Sabine, were born into a well-known and educated family in Breslau, Germany, in 1906. His father, Karl Bonhoeffer, became a famous psychiatrist and neurologist in Berlin, where the family of ten moved in 1912. A few years later, Dietrich's oldest brother, Walter, was killed fighting for Germany in World War I.

At the age of fourteen, Dietrich declared that he wanted to be "a theologian." This came as a surprise to his family, who, although Lutheran, rarely went to church. But Dietrich was quite serious and studied theology at the University of Berlin and, later, at Union Theological Seminary in New York.

As part of his practical experience as a pastor, Dietrich Bonhoeffer spent time working with the poor and out-of-work in Barcelona, Spain; worshiping with a black Baptist church in Harlem, New York; and teaching a confirmation class for slum children in Berlin. These experiences helped Bonhoeffer look at the

Gospel "from below," from the view of people who suffer.

In the meantime, Hitler was rising to power in Germany. Reclaiming their national identity and power after World War I fueled the German people—even many Christians—to accept Nazism without question. But Dietrich Bonhoeffer clearly saw the danger and helped to form the "Confessing Church." It proclaimed that Jesus alone is Lord and that loyalty to Hitler was idolatry. Along with six thousand other pastors, he refused to accept the "Aryan Clause" that discriminated against anyone of Jewish descent.

Soon he became involved in a resistance movement to overthrow Hitler. His activities led to his arrest by the Gestapo in 1943. On April 9, 1945, he was hanged with several other resisters—only a few weeks before Hitler committed suicide and Germany surrendered to the Allies. But his writings, such as *The Cost of Discipleship*, *Life Together*, and *Letters and Papers From Prison* continue to challenge Christians today.

LOYALTY
A German in Harlem

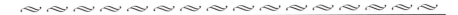

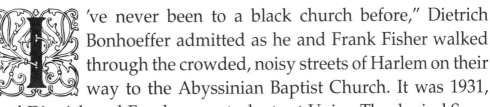've never been to a black church before," Dietrich Bonhoeffer admitted as he and Frank Fisher walked through the crowded, noisy streets of Harlem on their way to the Abyssinian Baptist Church. It was 1931, and Dietrich and Frank were students at Union Theological Seminary in New York. Frank, a committed black Christian from Alabama, was doing his fieldwork for seminary at the church, and Dietrich had asked to go along.

Frank shrugged. He wondered how long this blond-haired, ruddy-faced seminary student who spoke English with a thick German accent would last when he got to know the real Harlem. But to Frank's surprise, Dietrich came back each week, volunteered to teach Sunday school, and visited in Harlem homes. Dietrich listened and tried to see American life through the eyes of his new friends.

As friendship grew between the black American and the white German, Frank shared some of his own experiences growing up in a segregated country, where people of different races were kept apart. Dietrich asked a lot of questions about the poor schools and housing, as well as the lack of good jobs for blacks. Wasn't every person in democratic America supposed to have an equal opportunity to go to a good school or have a good job?

"Why doesn't the church do something about these problems?" he asked. Frank could only shake his head.

One day, Dietrich and Frank and a few other fellows from the seminary went out to a restaurant to eat. The waiter took orders from the young white men but ignored Frank. When Dietrich realized what was happening, he stood up in disgust. "If Frank cannot get service here, none of us will eat here." And he led the group out of the restaurant.

When Dietrich's year at Union Theological Seminary was over, it was time to go home to Germany. Frank shook his friend's hand and said, "Make our sufferings known in Germany. Tell them what is happening to us, and show them what we are like."

Back in Germany, Dietrich remembered his promise to Frank. He had recorded some of the music from the Abyssinian Baptist Church, including some black spirituals. He played this music for his students and talked about the injustice for blacks he had seen in America, even among people who worshiped the same Jesus. "Racism," he predicted, "will become one of the biggest future problems for the white church."

Little did Dietrich Bonhoeffer realize how true his words would become—not only between blacks and whites in America, but between "Aryans" and Jews in Germany. But the seeds of justice had already been planted in his heart, so when Hitler set out to destroy all Jews, Dietrich refused to turn against them.

Loyalty means standing up for fellow Christians and others who are suffering injustice.

FROM GOD'S WORD:

A friend loves you all the time, and a brother helps in time of trouble (Proverbs 17:17).

LET'S TALK ABOUT IT:

1. Why do you think Dietrich Bonhoeffer, a white German Christian, thought it was important to get to know a black American Christian?
2. In what ways did Bonhoeffer show his loyalty to Frank?
3. Why is it sometimes hard to be loyal to someone that other people ignore or don't like?

TRUTH
"Church, Remain a Church!"

~~~~~~

ietrich Bonhoeffer and his friend Franz Hildebrandt were worried. Both young men had gone to seminary and wanted to become pastors. But by 1933, more and more Protestant church leaders were praising Hitler, Germany's powerful leader. "It is because of Hitler that Christ has become effective among us!" one church leader said. "National Socialism [Nazism] is positive Christianity in action!"

"That's idolatry!" Dietrich exclaimed to his friend. "These 'German Christians,' as they call themselves, are confusing Germanism with Christianity. What are we going to do?"

"There are going to be elections at the national church council in July," Franz said. "Maybe we can convince delegates sent by the churches not to vote for church leaders who support Hitler."

Dietrich and Franz talked to many delegates about their concerns. Just before the churchwide elections that summer, Dietrich preached a strong sermon: "Church, remain a church!" he pleaded. "Confess, confess, confess!" He meant that the church should tell people that only Jesus is Lord and that Christians must be followers of Christ, not Hitler.

In spite of the hard work of young reformers like Dietrich, the church council elected a Nazi sympathizer as national bishop. And only two months later, many church leaders showed up at another council wearing brown Nazi uniforms and giving the Nazi salute. The "Brown Synod," as it was nicknamed, adopted the Aryan Clause, which said that no one with Jewish blood could become a Christian pastor.

Dietrich was stunned. His friend Franz was a Jewish Christian!

It was getting dangerous to speak against the government, but Dietrich wasn't going to give up on the truth so easily. "If the so-called German 'Christians' support Hitler," he argued, "then we must help Christians like us stand against these anti-Jewish rules." Bonhoeffer and others helped collect the signatures of two thousand pastors who promised to fight to reverse the Aryan Clause.

The new bishop, however, ignored the petition.

"Whether we are successful or not, we must still stand for the truth," Dietrich encouraged the other pastors. In May of 1934, this group formed the "Confessing Church." They adopted the Barmen Confession of Faith, which stated: "We [reject] the false teaching that there are areas of our life in which we belong not to Jesus Christ but to other lords."

The "other lords" referred to Hitler. Everyone knew what these daring pastors were saying: that promising loyalty to Hitler was idolatry. It meant making Hitler more important than Jesus Christ. Dietrich Bonhoeffer also knew that by signing this confession, he and his fellow pastors had become "enemies of the state." The Gestapo—Hitler's secret police—would be watching them.

Truth must be defended against lies, but it might cost us something.

FROM GOD'S WORD:

They traded the truth of God for a lie. They worshiped and served what had been created instead of the God who created those things, who should be praised forever. Amen (Romans 1:25).

LET'S TALK ABOUT IT:

1. The Nazi government thought the church leaders who supported Hitler were patriotic and working for the "good" of their country. Was Bonhoeffer unpatriotic by going against these church leaders?
2. What was wrong about the Aryan Clause?
3. What "truths" might other people think are "unpatriotic" in our own country?

PEACE
Double Agent . . . and Pastor

~~~~~~~~~~~~~~~~~~~~~~~~~~~~~~~~~~

The Nazi guard at the border between Germany and Switzerland looked at the papers Dietrich Bonhoeffer handed him. "So. You are an agent in the *Abwehr*— military intelligence," said the guard. He glared into the car. "Who are these others?"

"Civilian agents with the Abwehr on special assignment," said Dietrich casually, leaning against the car, hands in his pockets. "It's all there in the papers."

"How long will you be staying in Switzerland?" the guard pressed.

"That, sir, is secret Abwehr business," said Dietrich pointedly, getting back in the car. "May we go through now?"

With a shrug, the guard handed the papers back through the open car window and lifted the barrier so the car could go through. A few miles down the road, the fearful people in the car began to relax. Dietrich grinned. "Well," he joked to his relieved passengers, who were all German Jews, "smuggling Jews into Switzerland is secret business, right?"

What Pastor Bonhoeffer was doing was risky. Part of what he said was true: He *was* an Abwehr agent, supposedly using his church contacts outside Germany to get information about the political situation in other countries. But in reality he was a double agent—delivering news to the Allies (especially Britain) about the plot to overthrow Hitler. Sometimes he was able to use his position to smuggle Jews out of Germany.

But on April 29, 1943, the Gestapo caught up with Dietrich and arrested him. For two years, he was in prison and Nazi concentration camps, not knowing whether he would be put to death for treason or freed by the approaching Allied armies.

In prison, however, Dietrich once again became what he was at heart: a pastor. Because of his first-aid training, he was called when any of the prisoners became sick or were injured in the air raids. This gave him a chance to give spiritual comfort as well. He wrote letters to his family and friends (which were later published), sharing his thoughts about being a Christian in hard times. Even the guards noticed that Dietrich seemed calm and peaceful, and some of them shared their problems with him and asked him to pray for them.

One Sunday after Easter, he preached an enouraging sermon to his fellow prisoners at the extermination camp of Slössenberg, on Isaiah 53:5: "By his stripes we are healed" (KJV). Even in their troubles, he said, Christ's resurrection from the dead gave them hope. That same day, Dietrich got the news: He was sentenced to be hanged the next day. Sending word to a friend, he said, "This is the end—for me, the beginning of life."

On the day of his execution, the prison doctor saw Dietrich kneel down on the floor of his cell, praying. Later, the doctor said, "I was most deeply moved by the way this lovable man prayed, so devout and so certain that God heard his prayer. At the place of execution, he again said a prayer. . . . In the almost fifty years that I worked as a doctor, I have hardly ever seen a man die so entirely submissive to the will of God."

It was April 9, 1945—only one month before Germany surrendered to the Allies.

The peace of God that we share with others also gives us strength in hard times.

FROM GOD'S WORD:

And God's peace, which is so great we cannot understand it, will keep your hearts and minds in Christ Jesus (Philippians 4:7).

LET'S TALK ABOUT IT:

1. In what ways did Dietrich Bonhoeffer bring God's peace to Jews who were being persecuted? to other prisoners? to the prison guards?
2. What was the source of Bonhoeffer's peaceful spirit?
3. God's peace is the best, most true peace there is. Do you experience and feel the peace of God? In what way?

JOHN BUNYAN

———— ⟨⟨⟨ ————

The Pilgrim Who Made Progress

John Bunyan was born in 1628 in a small town in southern England. He was the son of a tinker, someone who fixed pots and pans, sharpened knives, and did other small metal work. That became John's work, too, but he also started preaching.

When John was young, England was torn by civil war. King Charles I was killed, and his son, Charles II, was driven out of the country. Oliver Cromwell then took over the government. He ruled well, but when he died, Charles II was brought back and made king.

When the kings were in power, the official Church of England controlled most religious life and supported the king. But when Oliver Cromwell ruled, he encouraged the independent churches—Puritan, Baptist, Presbyterian, and Quaker. Naturally, when King Charles II returned to power, he wanted to get rid of these independent churches. He feared that they might be disloyal to him.

But it was in these independent churches that John Bunyan preached. When he was told to stop, he refused to obey the king's law. He said he had to obey God. So he was thrown into prison.

After giving birth to four children, John's first wife died in about 1658, the same year that Oliver Cromwell died. John was very lonely and needed help raising his small children. Mary, the oldest, was only eight years old and blind. Before long, John remarried. Elizabeth, his new wife, became a loving wife and mother and bore two more children.

The prison where John was sent in 1661 was just down the street from the Bunyan home, and every day his blind daughter, Mary, brought him a jug of soup.

Bunyan spent nearly twelve years in prison, but he did not waste his time. He wrote many articles and books. The most well-known book is *Pilgrim's Progress*, an imaginary story of a young man traveling toward heaven. John was released from prison in 1672 and returned to his life as a pastor.

He died in London in 1688 from pneumonia, which he apparently caught after riding through a chilling rainstorm to help settle an argument between a father and son.

COURAGE
The Chance to Escape Not Taken

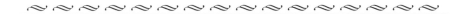

ohn Bunyan turned up his coat collar against the sharp autumn wind as he climbed the hill to the familiar farm not far from Harlington. He had made the thirteen-mile walk from his home in Bedford, eager to meet with the faithful Christians who often gathered under the beautiful trees on the hill to hear him preach.

But on that twelfth of November in 1660, it was too cold for an outdoor meeting, so everyone had gathered inside the farmhouse.

John went in smiling at everyone, but his old friends did not greet him with the same warmth they usually did. Instead, they turned away and talked quietly among themselves.

Finally, a farmer drew Bunyan aside and said, "John, we've heard that there is a warrant out for your arrest. But all these common people like you, so our local policeman is not eager to arrest you. In fact, he told me he wouldn't be here for another hour. So you have plenty of time to slip away."

"Slip away?" said Bunyan. "Why would I do that? I haven't

done anything wrong. We're not planning some kind of a revolution here." Then Bunyan raised his voice so everyone in the room could hear him. "Good people, cheer up. We have no reason to be ashamed of gathering here to worship the Lord. And as for me, preaching God's Word is a good work. One day, I will be rewarded for it, so why should I care if I must suffer a little now?"

There were still a few minutes before the meeting was to begin, so Bunyan went outside to pray as he walked under the tall elm trees in the setting sun. He had known this day would come. Earlier, the British government had passed a law saying only official church ministers could preach. John was not part of the official church, so he knew that if he continued to preach, he would someday be arrested. Tonight might be the night. He could run, but if he did so out of fear, what would happen to the new believers? They would give up hope—and their faith. No! He would not quit.

Back inside the farmhouse, all had arrived and were ready for the service. John began.

In a few minutes, two more people slipped in the door and stood at the back. They were the local policeman and his assistant. As they watched, they saw that these people had no weapons. They were not speaking against the government or planning a revolution. He did not see why he had to arrest this tinker just because he was preaching. But on the other hand, he had his orders, so he went forward and did his job.

The people were alarmed when Bunyan was arrested.

"Don't worry, folks," Bunyan said. "Thank God that we were not arrested for doing something wrong. Instead, we suffer as Christians for doing what is right. It is better to suffer than to make others suffer."

With that, the policeman took Bunyan away to prison, where he spent the next twelve years.

Courage is needed to do what is right even when you might suffer for it.

FROM GOD'S WORD:
Be alert. Continue strong in the faith. Have courage, and be strong (1 Corinthians 16:13).

LET'S TALK ABOUT IT:
1. Why didn't John Bunyan take the chance to escape when he had it?
2. What might have happened to the new believers or weaker Christians if Bunyan had fled?
3. Why is courage important for us today? Tell about a time when you might need courage.

TRUST

Leaving Mary in Jesus' Hands

~~~~~~~~~~~~~~~~~~~~~~~~~~~~~~~~~~~~~

ou can get out any time you want to," Paul Cobb said to John Bunyan as the two sat talking in Bunyan's prison cell in his hometown of Bedford. Paul Cobb was Bedford's Clerk of the Peace. "All you have to do," he continued, "is promise not to preach anymore. We know you aren't a revolutionary, but the king is . . . well, he's not taking any chances."

John stood up, walked over to the door of his cell, and looked through the bars. He had never imagined he would be in prison for more than a few days. But days had turned into weeks and weeks into months. How much worse would it get?

Lately, nightmares had troubled his sleep. In his dreams, he saw the gallows outside town where criminals were sometimes hung. He imagined that his body was hanging there, swinging in the rain. Such nightmares were very frightening, and he often woke up in a cold sweat praying for the courage to remain faithful to God.

Slowly, God had given him that courage, and the nightmares

stopped. He no longer feared for his own life and safety. "No," Bunyan answered Paul Cobb. "I cannot make such a promise. The Scriptures tell us we must obey God rather than man, and God has clearly commanded us to preach the Gospel. I could never promise not to do that, not even to get out of this dark hole."

When Cobb left, there was another visitor for Bunyan. It was his oldest daughter, Mary. She came almost every day to deliver a jug of soup, and her visits brought John great joy. But lately, he had been worrying about her. She was about eleven years old and had been blind from birth. And yet she had learned to bravely walk the streets of Bedford. Now she had no trouble bringing the jug of soup the few blocks from the Bunyan home to the prison where her father was.

But what will happen to her? worried Bunyan. *She needs special help and protection.* He thought about the cruel children of the village who would likely tease and trick her because of her blindness. He worried about how she could make a living when she grew up. *What if she has to beg for food or is beaten or lives in the cold? Who will take care of her if I'm in prison or if I die?*

He loved her so much that he could hardly hold back his tears until after she left. "Oh, Lord, I no longer care about myself," he cried out to God, falling to his knees on the cold stone floor. "But what should I do about my family? Am I to risk them and make their lives harder? What about my poor, blind daughter? It seems too much."

Then into his mind came the image of Jesus taking the children onto His knee and saying, "Let the little children come to me, and do not hinder them, for the kingdom of heaven belongs to such as these" (Matthew 19:14, NIV).

At last, Bunyan's heart found peace. He would trust Jesus to take care of his dear Mary even when he couldn't be there for her.

And Jesus did keep Mary safe through all the years John spent in prison.

Trusting Jesus means believing that He will keep His promises—all of them.

FROM GOD'S WORD:
Jesus said, "Don't let your hearts be troubled. Trust in God, and trust in me" (John 14:1).

LET'S TALK ABOUT IT:
1. Why wouldn't John Bunyan promise not to preach?
2. As long as Bunyan was in prison, he couldn't protect and care for his daughter. Why did he worry about her? What did he do?
3. What should we do when things are beyond our control?

CREATIVITY
The Jailhouse Preacher

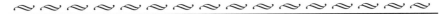

n prison, there were not many pots and pans for a tinker like John Bunyan to repair. And the jailer certainly wasn't going to allow a prisoner to make or sharpen knives. So what could a tinker like John do with his time?

"You know, there is a need for more laces in the clothing business," a visitor told Bunyan one day. "All the fancy clothes makers in London need them. If you could make me some good, quality laces, I would sell them for you. It wouldn't bring much money, but it might help support your family."

John was delighted. He was good with crafts. Finally, here was something that used his skill with his hands.

He got a bench to work on and set it up in the corner of the prison's common room. Then he asked the jailer to allow him to order some thin cord and small pieces of brass. He cut the cord to its proper length and, with a pair of pliers, squeezed the brass tabs onto each end of the cord so the tips of the cord wouldn't unravel.

Over and over again he did this task until he had piles of the laces. These he bundled and sold for a few pennies to give to his family. The work also gave him a creative way to use his skill with his hands even in prison.

But what about his gift for preaching?

Sometimes he preached to the other prisoners, and sometimes he stood at one of the barred prison windows and preached to people on the street. But God had called him to share the Gospel with all people. He needed a better way.

The apostle Paul had written books or letters from prison— why couldn't he? So John began writing sermons and sending them out to be published. In one of the first ones, he explained why he was in prison. In another he talked about heaven, and in another about hell. As he wrote, he got an idea for a story that would interest young and old alike. Maybe he even tried out his stories on his children when they came to visit. *Pilgrim's Progress*, as the story was called, became his most popular work. People all over the English-speaking world read it and still read it today.

Bunyan's story is about becoming a Christian, the struggles we have with doubt and fear and other problems, and our reward in heaven. But Bunyan didn't just talk about these truths like he was preaching a sermon. He tried something more creative. He imagined this was the journey of a young pilgrim traveling through dangerous country, fighting dragons, fleeing giants, and escaping swamps. Along the way, the pilgrim met faithful companions and cowardly fakers, but he kept safe from harm whenever he put on the armor of God. The exciting journey ends when Pilgrim at last arrives in the heavenly city. The adventure of *Pilgrim's Progress* is still loved today.

By using the creativity God had given him, John Bunyan made his years in prison useful. Not only was he able to support himself and his family, but he also continued the ministry God had asked him to do: Preach the Gospel!

Creativity is using the abilities and gifts God has given us to do the work He has assigned us.

FROM GOD'S WORD:

I have become all things to all people so I could save some of them in any way possible (1 Corinthians 9:22b).

LET'S TALK ABOUT IT:

1. Why did John Bunyan make laces in prison? Why did he start writing books from prison?
2. How was making laces and writing books a creative use of John's God-given abilities and gifts?
3. Name two things you can do well. Can you think of a new, creative way one of those things might someday be used to serve God? How?

PETER CARTWRIGHT

The Two-Fisted Preacher

As the American frontier moved west, there were seldom enough families in the wilderness to support a local minister. So preachers known as circuit riders traveled from place to place visiting families. Whenever they could gather a handful of people, they held a church service. Often, it took them four to six weeks to "ride a circuit."

About once a year, families from neighboring circuits gathered for a camp meeting, an outdoor conference noted for great singing, bold preaching, and religious excitement.

One colorful and successful circuit rider was Peter Cartwright. At age fifteen, he was dramatically converted from a life of gambling, fighting, and horse racing. Two years later, in 1802, the leaders of Peter's Methodist Episcopal Church in Kentucky asked him to create a new circuit in the unchurched wilderness three counties west. This was the beginning of his riding the trail for fifty-three years over tens of thousands of miles. In so doing, he brought the Gospel to frontier families in Kentucky, Tennessee, Indiana, Ohio, and Illinois.

Peter Cartwright preached the Gospel boldly and wouldn't allow any troublemakers to disrupt his camp meetings. If he couldn't outwit them, he would physically kick them out. And at a stocky two hundred pounds, Peter could do it.

One of his great sorrows was the increase in slavery among church families. When he began preaching, there was a church rule in Kentucky against ministers having slaves, but as time passed, there were more and more exceptions to the rule. Cartwright feared it would split the church, which it did some years later. When he felt that he could no longer fight successfully against this trend, he moved his family and ministry to the free state of Illinois. There he became friends with Abraham Lincoln.

He died at his farm in Pleasant Plains, Illinois, on September 25, 1872, just after his eighty-seventh birthday.

DISCERNMENT
Catching the Trickster

~~~~~~~~~~~~~~~~~~~~~~~~~~~~~~~~~~~~~~

Peter Cartwright had just started camp meetings in Marietta, Ohio, when a strange character showed up. "My name is Halcyon," he announced gravely. "I am a messenger from God." Bragging about himself, he claimed to see visions and fall into trances where he talked with angels.

Peter Cartwright didn't like religious fakes. They upset his camp meetings and tried to trick uneducated frontier people out of their money. So Cartwright was immediately suspicious and wouldn't let the man preach or take up an offering for what Halcyon claimed was "God's work." Cartwright also decided to keep an eye on this fellow.

Sure enough, when it got dark, the man snuck away and lit a cigar. Then he took a small bag of gunpowder down near the river and dumped it into an old, hollowed-out tree stump. He touched the cigar to the powder . . . suddenly, there was a loud *varoom*, and a brilliant flash could be seen throughout the camp. When the powder exploded, Halcyon fell to the ground with his eyes closed as though he were in a trance.

In a few moments, a large crowd had gathered to see what had happened. Halcyon "came to," fluttering his eyelids. "Ohh," he moaned, "I've just received a message from God."

But when Cartwright arrived with a lantern, he smelled sulfur (which smells like burning matches) and noticed the cigar butt nearby in the grass. These clues gave him a pretty good idea of what had happened.

"Forget about these Methodist camp meetings," Halcyon was telling the people. "If you follow me, God will—"

Peter stepped forward and interrupted. "Excuse me, sir. Did an angel just appear to you in a flash of light?"

"He most certainly did, brother. And he gave me a message for all these good people."

Peter wrinkled his nose and sniffed the still evening air. "Mr. Halcyon, did this angel smell like brimstone?" (Brimstone is another word for burning sulfur.)

Possibly Halcyon's nose was stuffed up and he couldn't smell. "Why do you ask me such a foolish question?" he said. "Only hell smells of brimstone."

"That's strange," said Peter. "Because I smell sulfur. Come on over here, folks, and have a look at this stump. Whoever left such a scorch on this stump must have been from what the Bible calls the lake of fire and brimstone—hell itself. And my, oh my," Peter said, shining his light toward the grass. "He must have been smoking a cigar, too, 'cause look at this butt here in the grass."

The people began to laugh and walk away. They'd almost been tricked, but the trickster had been caught instead.

Discernment is the good sense to recognize the difference between truth and error.

FROM GOD'S WORD:

My child, hold on to wisdom and good sense [or discernment]. Don't let them out of your sight (Proverbs 3:21).

LET'S TALK ABOUT IT:

1. Why do you think Halcyon wanted to get the people away from following Peter Cartwright?
2. What did Peter Cartwright notice that tipped him off that this man was a fake?
3. Sometimes tricks are just for fun, but can you think of a time when someone played a trick on you that made you feel bad? Describe it.

JUSTICE
The Joy of Doing Right

As the singing that had opened the Kentucky camp meeting faded into the trees, a square-faced, curly-headed man got up to preach. On the hard benches below the rustic platform, Brother and Sister Stewart eagerly opened their Bibles and listened. Camp meetings were always fun, and tonight they would hear the famous Peter Cartwright.

But when Cartwright began to preach, the Stewarts became troubled.

"The Bible says," shouted Peter in order to be heard by the crowd, " 'Love your neighbor as yourself.' Think about this, my friends. Would you like to be treated like a piece of property? Would you like to be bought and sold and have no freedom? Yet that is how people treat slaves. You slave owners, are you treating these slaves as you would like to be treated? Are you obeying God?"

His words cut deep because even though the Stewarts were sincere Christian people, they owned several slaves.

All week long, many people prayed for the joy of the Lord to fill their hearts. And when God answered that prayer, they shouted and sang and thanked Him for this gift. But whenever Mrs. Stewart prayed, all she could think about was the unhappy life of her slaves.

She got down on her knees between the old log benches in the camp meeting and prayed harder, but still she felt no joy. Finally, she made God a promise: "If You will give me joy, we will give up our slaves and set them free."

Immediately, God filled her heart with such great joy that she didn't know whether she was dreaming or awake. She rose from her knees and shouted to the crowd around her, "I've received the gift of joy! Thank God, He's given me joy!"

Then she told them about the promise she'd made to God. There was such power in her words that hundreds of people fell to the ground praising God. That afternoon, many people became new Christians, and many long-time Christians repented and asked forgiveness for keeping slaves, too.

Cartwright believed that showing people what was right and wrong from God's Word was the best way to oppose slavery. He said this kind of preaching had freed hundreds and thousands of slaves. In most cases, the owners were encouraged to offer their former slaves a choice. The former slaves could either have some land and money to get started on their own, or they could have enough money to take a ship and move back to Africa. (At this time, they probably would have gone to the colony of Liberia.)

This kind of repentance and love often led former slaves to accept Christ as Savior, too. In addition, former slaves and former slave owners frequently became friends, a real witness to God's healing for past sin.

Within a few days after the Kentucky camp meeting where Mrs. Stewart received the joy of the Lord, the Stewarts and several other families set their slaves free. In doing so, their joy spread to many black families.

Justice requires doing what is right, even when it costs you something.

FROM GOD'S WORD:
Stop doing wrong, learn to do right! Seek justice, encourage the oppressed. Defend the cause of the fatherless, plead the case of the widow (Isaiah 1:16b–17, NIV).

LET'S TALK ABOUT IT:
1. Why was Mrs. Stewart at first unable to experience the joy of the Lord?
2. Why did Peter Cartwright think the best way to free slaves was to use God's Word?
3. Tell about a time when you had to sacrifice or give up something in order to do what was right. How did you feel after doing it?

HUMOR
The Cornstalk Duel

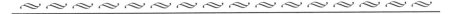

rom the platform at the front of the camp meeting, Peter Cartwright announced, "I'm sorry, gentlemen, that side is reserved for the ladies. Would you kindly move over to the men's side?"

The boys seated on the ladies' side had placed themselves behind some girls with whom they were flirting. Most moved quickly. But a few ducked down and tried to hide.

That didn't fool Cartwright. He cleared his throat and boomed, "Thank you, *gentlemen*. Now let's see how many *clowns* we have left." He pointed toward the wayward boys and said, "I see one right there on the end of row ten. Would you please stand up? Yes, you, young man—you in the brown jacket. Stand up and take a bow."

The boy sheepishly came to his feet.

"What's the matter, young man? Are you not able to tell the difference between the gentlemen and the ladies in this crowd? It seems pretty easy to me. The ladies are the ones wearing the dresses. Now, you wouldn't be hiding a dress under those long pants of yours, would you?"

The crowd roared with laughter, especially the girls in row nine.

With that, the boy's neck and cheeks became bright red, and he turned and ran for the back. The other boys followed, stooping over like they were trying to hide behind a hedge. When the crowd's laughter finally died down, the camp meeting began.

The next day, Peter Cartwright was invited to dinner at a nearby home. Also present was the father of the boy in the brown jacket. However, the man had not been at the camp meeting the night before. He had only heard about what had happened from his son. "You shouldn't have embarrassed my boy in public," he said with anger.

"Sir, anyone with manners could have seen that one side was for gentlemen and the other for ladies. I gave the boys a chance to move. Only the stubborn ones refused. They were making fools of themselves. I only pointed it out, which was what they deserved."

"How dare you?" roared the man as he stood up, nearly knocking over his chair. "If you weren't such a coward, I would challenge you to a duel."

Peter Cartwright took another bite of biscuit and then, without looking up, said very calmly, "Sir, if you challenge me, I will accept."

"Then I challenge you to mortal combat!"

A fight to the death! The guests around the table became silent. Not one fork moved. No one chewed—except Peter Cartwright. Everyone was staring at the two men.

"Very well," said Cartwright. "But according to the rules of honor, I have the right to choose our weapons. Is that not so?"

"Of course."

"Then, let us go outside and grab a couple of cornstalks and have at it with 'em. I think that ought to settle things quite well enough. Don't you?" And he smiled broadly with his big, crooked grin.

At first, the man clenched his fists and looked as though he would explode, but then he realized that Cartwright had just given him a humorous way to get out of making a fool of himself. The anger melted from his face. He laughed nervously. Then everyone joined in the laughter, and the whole thing was over.

At the next camp meeting, the man became a Christian.

Humor is a way to melt tension and hard feelings.

FROM GOD'S WORD:
A happy heart is like good medicine, but a broken spirit drains your strength (Proverbs 17:22).

LET'S TALK ABOUT IT:
1. Why did the boys sit on the ladies' side? Do you think they knew better?
2. How did Cartwright end a tense moment with the boy's father?
3. Describe a time when someone you know used humor to cool down another person's anger.

JIM ELLIOT

―――――――――― ❧⌒❧ ――――――――――

A Modern Martyr for
Stone-Age Indians

To the casual observer at the midpoint of the twentieth century, Jim Elliot might have seemed like an ordinary, bright, clean-cut, all-American boy. He had good looks, knew how to work hard, got good grades, wrestled in college, fell in love with an attractive young woman student, and could easily have achieved "the American dream" of a successful career and family.

But Jim Elliot was anything but ordinary.

Born in Portland, Oregon, in 1927, Jim accepted Christ as his Savior at age six. Growing up in a loving, deeply religious home, Jim developed a faith that was a part of his daily life. By the time he went to Wheaton College, in Wheaton, Illinois, in 1945 at age eighteen, he had one burning desire: to know God and serve Him with his whole being. For Jim, this meant the probability of a life of service and sacrifice on the mission field.

He met Elisabeth Howard at Wheaton College, but hesitated to ask her to marry him until God showed him the direction for his life and whether God wanted him to marry or remain single. After graduation and a two-year "waiting" period, Jim knew where God was leading him: to Ecuador to translate the Scriptures for Indian tribes who had never heard about Jesus.

In 1952, Jim sailed for Ecuador. In 1953, Elisabeth joined him and became his wife. God was bringing together a very special team of missionaries—including Ed McCully, Pete Fleming, Roger Youderian, pilot Nate Saint, and their wives—for a special assignment: to reach the fierce, stone-age Auca Indian tribe with the Gospel.

But within days of the first personal contact with the Aucas, the five men were dead. On January 8, 1956, Jim and his friends literally poured out their lives to spread the Gospel. Some might call it a tragedy, a waste—yet their deaths were seeds that have sprouted and grown everlasting fruit.

JOY
A Boyhood Dream

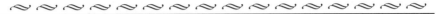

oung Jimmy Elliot squinted hard at the tiny drawing of a ship's sails in the huge dictionary. "Flying jib . . . foresail . . . mainsail . . ." he muttered to himself, trying to memorize all the different sails.

"Finding what you're looking for?" asked the school librarian, peering over his shoulder.

Jimmy's face reddened. "Yes, ma'am," he said, hoping she would lose interest and go away. As the librarian moved on, Jimmy shut his eyes, letting his dream drift back into his mind. The grammar school in Portland, Oregon, faded from reality, and he was standing on the deck of a plunging ship, watching the sails above him snap and fill with the ocean winds. The boy imagined himself a sailor, expertly tightening the ropes that held the sails, then taking his turn at the big wooden wheel that guided the rudder beneath the waves. . . .

Fourteen years later, on February 4, 1952, twenty-four-year-old Jim Elliot and his companion, Pete Fleming, watched from the deck of the *Santa Juana* as their 2,300 pounds of supplies and luggage were loaded on board the cargo ship. Below him on the dock at San Pedro, California, stood his parents, waving good-bye and looking a bit teary eyed. But all Jim could feel was excitement. He and Pete were on their way to South America at last!

In the years between Jim's boyhood dream and his voyage on the *Santa Juana*, Jim had graduated from high school, then gone on to Wheaton College in Wheaton, Illinois. The more Jim Elliot studied his Bible, the more he had a deep desire to know God and to serve Him with his whole life.

But what did God want him to do? What was God's will for Jim Elliot? Jim grew more and more certain that, for him, serving God meant sharing the Gospel with people who had never heard about Jesus before. But even after he graduated from college, God still hadn't shown him what country or *which* people. So he prayed . . . and waited.

And then he heard about the Quichua (*keech-wah*) people in Ecuador and the need for missionaries to help translate the Quichua language into written form so they could have God's Word in their own language. Now Jim knew what God wanted him to do—take the Gospel to the unreached tribes of Ecuador in South America.

Jim stood on the deck of the *Santa Juana*, watching as the winter sun set on the Pacific Ocean after their first day at sea. Pete Fleming gave a little groan and patted his stomach. "Are they going to feed us like this all the way to Ecuador?" he complained good-naturedly. "What a meal! Black cod, potatoes au gratin, fresh salad, good coffee . . ."

Jim smiled. But he wasn't thinking about the food. "When I was a boy," he said to Pete, "I used to dream about going to sea. Now here I am on board ship—as a passenger, not a sailor—but it's thrilling just the same. I had no idea that God would grant me a taste of my dream if I followed His will."

Inside, Jim was nearly bursting with joy. But what was that joy? Fulfilling his boyhood dream of going to sea? No, Jim realized, this joy was much bigger and deeper than that. He sat down in his cabin and wrote to his parents that he was feeling ". . . the sheer joy of being in the will of God and the knowledge of His direction [for my life]."

Joy comes when we know God's will and do it.

FROM GOD'S WORD:
You have made known to me the path of life; you will fill me with joy in your presence (Psalm 16:11, NIV).

LET'S TALK ABOUT IT:
1. What did Jim Elliot want to do when he was a boy? What did he want to do by the time he got to college?
2. Doing *what* gave Jim Elliot the greatest joy?
3. How do you feel when you know God wants you to do something and you do it?

PATIENCE
Operation Auca

on Carlos shook his head at his visitor. "You want to know what the Auca Indians are like? Savage, stone-age killers, that's what! If I were you, Señor Elliot, I'd stay far away from them. If you don't believe me, talk to Dayuma, the Auca woman who works for me. She escaped from the tribe a few years back."

Jim Elliot looked thoughtfully at the rich Ecuadoran farmer. He didn't dare tell Don Carlos that he and four other missionaries were planning to make contact with the Aucas and hopefully win their friendship. It was a crazy idea—everyone said it was impossible. But Jim and the others had a secret goal: to share the Gospel with the Aucas in their own language.

At Jim's request, Dayuma taught the young missionary several helpful words and phrases in the Auca language. "But," she warned, "do not trust them. To you they might seem friendly for a while, but they will not stop short of killing."

When Jim told the other missionaries what Dayuma had said, they nodded soberly. It might have been tempting to give up their plan right then, but Pete Fleming voiced the thought that kept them going: "Savage, stone-age killers who have never been reached by the Gospel before need the message of God's redeeming love more than many others."

In September 1955, Nate Saint and Ed McCully, two of the missionaries, had seen a cluster of Auca houses while flying in Nate's airplane. "From what we know of the Aucas, it's too dangerous to just go rushing into their village," Nate said. "Let's take a look at the whole area from the air, then slowly try to win their friendship."

The men agreed. "But," Jim reminded them, "if outside groups or the newspapers find out we're trying to reach the Aucas, curious people might hurry in. That would scare off the Aucas or get people killed. We must move slowly and keep our plan a secret."

More flights over the area showed several more Auca clearings. The first time Nate flew his plane low over the main clearing—which the missionaries nicknamed "Terminal City"—Auca Indians scattered in fright. But then the missionaries began dropping gifts tied to a rope: T-shirts, machetes, cloth, even pictures of the five men. Later, they were excited to see a few Aucas waving at the plane, and others wearing their gifts.

Nate flew as low as he dared, and the missionaries leaned out of the plane, calling out in the Auca language: "I like you! I am your friend!" Then something exciting happened. As Nate slowly circled the Auca clearing after dropping the rope, the Aucas tied on some gifts of their own: headbands of colorful feathers, and even a pet parrot!

Three months went by as the five missionaries tried to get the Auca people used to the small, yellow airplane flying over their villages. Finally in December, as Jim Elliot, Nate Saint, Ed McCully, Pete Fleming, and Roger Youderian got together to plan the next steps in Operation Auca, they made an important decision. It was time to actually meet the dangerous Aucas face-to-face. After all, their goal was to tell the Aucas the good news about Jesus—and meeting the Aucas in person was the only way.

Patience means being willing to wait or go slowly in order to reach the right goal.

FROM GOD'S WORD:
   It is better to finish something than to start it. It is better to be patient than to be proud (Ecclesiastes 7:8).

LET'S TALK ABOUT IT:
   1. Why was it important to keep Operation Auca a secret from the outside world?
   2. Why was it important to be patient and move ahead slowly and carefully?
   3. Share a goal you have that will take patience to finish.

SACRIFICE
"We've Made Contact!"

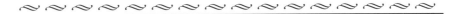

lisabeth Elliot was worried. "Are you sure this is the right time to contact the Aucas?" she asked Jim. "What will happen to the work we've started with the Quichuas?" Unspoken was the fear all the missionary wives shared: What if their husbands didn't come back?

Jim Elliot knew the real question behind his wife's doubts. He understood that he and the others were taking a big risk. But the Indian Christians they'd already taught could continue the work in Shandia. "I've been called," Jim told his wife simply.

The plans for meeting the Aucas face-to-face were made carefully, step by step. First the five missionaries would land on a strip of beach on the river nearest "Terminal City," the largest Auca village. Then the men would build a tree house for safety from jungle animals. They would wait for several days, letting the Aucas get used to their presence, before attempting to make contact.

On Tuesday, January 3, 1956, it took pilot Nate Saint five trips to fly in all five men and their supplies. The landings and take-offs on the beach were tricky, but their worst problem was the flying insects. The men got in touch with their wives each day, either by shortwave radio or with notes they sent with Nate in his plane. After a few days of camping on the beach, the men began calling Auca phrases of welcome across the river. Surely the Aucas were watching and listening. But would they come?

On Friday, the men were finally rewarded. An Auca man and two women appeared on the bank across from them. Jim Elliot waded into the river, using all the Auca phrases he knew, to help lead them safely across. It was an exciting day. The missionaries took pictures of the visit and even took the man, whom they nicknamed "George," up in the plane for a ride over his village.

Saturday, Nate and Pete flew back to base camp to pick up supplies and report the exciting news. They returned to the beach on Sunday morning. When they landed, Nate radioed back to his wife: "Pray for us! We're sure we'll have contact again today! Will radio you again at four-thirty."

Elisabeth Elliot and the other wives gathered eagerly around their radio. But four-thirty came and went. Nothing. When they still had not heard from the men by Monday morning, they knew something was wrong. A search party made its way to the river camp. Five bodies were found in the river. The men had been killed by Auca lances.

The tragic story soon appeared in newspapers around the world. Some people thought the five men were foolish to try to make friends with a savage Indian tribe. "A waste of lives!" they said. But hundreds of young people around the world, inspired by the dedication of Jim Elliot and the others, volunteered to become missionaries in their place. Eventually, Rachel Saint—Nate's sister—and Elisabeth Elliot lived among the very Aucas who had murdered the men. These women learned the Auca language and translated the Bible for them.

A waste? Jim Elliot wouldn't think so. He knew that Christians are sometimes called by God to "fall to the ground and die," like seeds, so that good fruit will grow. (See John 12:24.)

Sacrifice means a willingness to live—or die—for the cause of Christ.

FROM GOD'S WORD:
So brothers and sisters, since God has shown us great mercy, I beg you to offer your lives as a living sacrifice to him (Romans 12:1).

LET'S TALK ABOUT IT:
1. What do you think Jim Elliot meant when he told his wife, "I've been called"?
2. What were some of the good things that happened because of the deaths of these missionaries?
3. "Sacrifice" doesn't always (or even usually) mean death. In what ways might God be asking you to live sacrificially for Him?

ELIZABETH FRY

Angel of the Prisons

Quakers are Christians who believe in simple living, the brotherhood of all people, and working for peace instead of fighting wars.

Elizabeth Gurney was born May 21, 1780, into a Quaker family in Norwich, England. As a girl, Elizabeth often grumbled at the long, silent Quaker meetings. But at the age of eighteen, she turned her heart to God. When she decided to become a "Plain Friend"—wearing plain clothes and giving up the world's amusements—her sisters thought she was taking this "spiritual thing" too far.

Even after she married Joseph Fry and had a houseful of children, Elizabeth always found time to help the poor by bringing them warm clothing, medicine, and hot soup.

In 1813, Elizabeth visited Newgate Prison in London. The terrible conditions the prisoners lived in shocked her. So she formed the Ladies Newgate Committee, a group of Quaker volunteers who helped start a school for children of prisoners and supported many other prison reforms. People were amazed that Elizabeth always treated the prisoners with respect, kindness, and dignity.

Though she was often sick and had many family responsibilities, Elizabeth Fry kept on reaching out to the poor and the prisoners for the sake of Christ. Until her death in 1845 at the age of sixty-five, her prayer was always, "Whatever I do in anything, may I do it as to Thee."

RESPECT
Fanning the Spark

lizabeth Fry stepped into the crowded prison yard and almost lost her nerve. The horrible stink upset her stomach. Women were cursing each other, drinking gin, and gambling. Runny-nosed children clung to their mothers' skirts.

"Are you sure about this, missus?" asked the guard.

The Quaker woman swallowed her fear and said firmly, "Yes. Leave me alone with the prisoners."

Walking through the yard, Elizabeth talked first with one woman, then another. "I have a child about this one's age," she said, smiling. Or, "Such a strong lad! May I hold him?" Though plain, her gray silk dress seemed out of place next to the prisoners' rags. But the mothers mostly noticed her kind words.

After visiting awhile, Elizabeth opened her Bible to Matthew, chapter 20. As the women and children crowded around, she read the parable of the farmer who hired some workers in the morning, hired more at noon, and even hired a few one hour before quitting time! Then he generously paid them all the same wages.

After reading the story, she said, "You may think you have

wasted your life, but it isn't too late! God still offers mercy and forgiveness no matter when you come to Him."

Some of the women wept. No one had ever talked to them like this. Before she left, Elizabeth said, "Your children need an education. Choose someone here to be a teacher, and I will find school supplies."

The prisoners were surprised. This woman saw them as more than thieves and lawbreakers. It gave them hope.

Once the children were learning to read and write, Elizabeth realized the prisoners needed useful work—both to learn skills to use when they left prison, and because idle time led to drinking and fighting.

The prison officials didn't think it would work. "Look at the kind of people you're dealing with," they said. Still, a laundry room was turned into a workroom. Sewing supplies were given to the prisoners. A businessman agreed to sell items the women sewed. "But," Elizabeth told her new friends, "the rest is up to you. We haven't come here to boss you around. We will not make any rule or appoint any supervisor unless all of you agree."

Not once since they'd been in prison had anyone asked the women what they thought or gave them any responsibility. They accepted the challenge. Each rule and supervisor was voted on.

After a month of hard work, the women invited the prison officials for a visit. The visitors saw the women listening quietly while Mrs. Fry read Scripture. They noticed their improved behavior and orderly work. Impressed, the officials decided to use Mrs. Fry's reforms for the whole prison system. Maybe it was worth giving the prisoners a chance, after all!

"Of course," Elizabeth Fry agreed. "The spark of good is often smothered, but never wholly extinguished."

Respect means treating all people with kindness and dignity.

FROM GOD'S WORD:

" 'Lord, when did we see you hungry or thirsty or alone and away from home or without clothes or sick or in prison? When did we see these things and not help you?' Then the King will answer, 'I tell you the truth, anything you refused to do for even the least of my people here, you refused to do for me' " (Matthew 25:44–45).

LET'S TALK ABOUT IT:

1. Why do you think these rough prisoners listened to Elizabeth Fry?
2. What do you think Elizabeth Fry meant by her comment: "The spark of good is often smothered, but never wholly extinguished"?
3. It's hard to be around people who are rude and crude or sinful—much less be their friend! Do you know someone who's hard to like, but whom God wants you to treat with respect?

TRUTH
The Little Lost Book

Prison work kept Elizabeth Fry very busy, but she loved to visit her children and grandchildren. One day, Elizabeth noticed that her married daughter seemed tired and overworked. "Are you reading your Bible?" Elizabeth asked gently.

"Oh, Mama," cried her daughter, "I don't mean to neglect it, but I just don't have time!"

Elizabeth smiled to herself. She had given birth to eleven children. She knew how hard it could sometimes be to be a young mother! "That is exactly why I've written this book!" she said, laughing, as she pulled a small, red-leather book out of her bag. "I've selected short Scriptures for each day of the year—just right to tuck God's truth in the heart of busy mothers like you."

Just then Elizabeth heard a little voice at her elbow. "I want Grandmama's book, too," grandson Sammy said wistfully.

"Oh, Sammy, you can't even read yet!" protested his mother.

But Grandmama Elizabeth smiled. "Of course Sammy can have his own book!" She took another red book out of her bag and wrote on the inside, *To my precious Sammy, with love from Grand-mama—Elizabeth Fry.*

Sammy was so proud of his book. He carried it everywhere. He even carried it in his pocket one day when Papa took the children to the zoo. But as he ran around happily, the little red book fell out. When the loss was discovered hours later, Sammy was heartbroken. His own little "Bible," with his name written inside, was gone.

Everyone thought Sammy's book was lost forever. But a year later a clergyman told someone this story, which was passed along to Elizabeth Fry:

Another child visiting the zoo saw the little red book and picked it up. This boy had never had a book of his own, so he took it home. "Finders keepers," he bragged. The father of the boy was a thief. The mother wasn't much better, cursing God's name whenever she opened her mouth.

Everyone knew this family's wild reputation, so the clergyman was quite surprised to get a call one day from the local doctor, asking him to visit the woman, who was dying. "You will find the lion has become a lamb," the doctor said.

The woman was very sick. But her face glowed with peace. She welcomed the clergyman eagerly and asked him to pray with her. The clergyman was puzzled. "What has brought about this change in you?" he asked.

The woman reached under her pillow and pulled out Elizabeth Fry's red-leather book of daily Scripture readings. "The truth in this dear little book . . . my precious book," she whispered, "has taken away my fear of death."

Because the Word of God is true, it has the power to change lives.

FROM GOD'S WORD:
"The same thing is true of the words I speak. They will not return to me empty. They make the things happen that I want to happen, and they succeed in doing what I send them to do" (Isaiah 55:11).

LET'S TALK ABOUT IT:
1. Why do you think Elizabeth Fry wrote a book divided into short, daily Scriptures? Why didn't she just give Bibles away and tell people to read them?
2. How does Sammy's lost book illustrate the verse from Isaiah 55:11?
3. The apostle Paul said, "All Scripture is God-breathed and is useful for teaching, rebuking, correcting and training in righteousness" (2 Timothy 3:16, NIV). What are some ways you can "get the Word out" to others?

MERCY

A Bitter Good-Bye

ne day when Elizabeth arrived at the prison, many women were weeping. "What is the matter?" she cried.

"We've been exiled to Botany Bay!" they wailed. Botany Bay was a seaport on the other side of the world in a new colony called New South Wales, Australia. England thought sending people to live in these far-away colonies was a good way to get rid of criminals.

"They're loading us on the convict ships tomorrow!"

"What about our children? If they go with us, they might die! If they stay here—" Again the women wept at the thought of losing their children.

"What were your crimes?" Elizabeth asked. An old granny had stolen twelve pounds of cheese. One young woman had been sentenced to hang for stealing food; later her sentence was changed to exile in Australia. A thirteen-year-old stole a gown and bonnet worth seven shillings. She, too, was going to be exiled. Elizabeth knew what they did was wrong, but exile seemed like a very harsh punishment.

The next day, Elizabeth Fry came early to say good-bye to "her prisoners." But she was horrified by the circus mood of the city. The prisoners were chained with leg and wrist irons and crowded into open wagons. Jeering mobs lined the streets from the prison to the River Thames. As the wagons passed, people threw rotten vegetables at the prisoners and yelled, "Good riddance!" "Get rid of the criminals!" "England doesn't need scum like you!" When a rotten tomato found its mark, the crowd laughed with glee.

Vowing to do something about this cruel treatment, Elizabeth met with city officials. She pleaded with the Sheriffs of London, the Chaplain, and the Governor of the Prison for better treatment. By the summer of 1818, Mrs. Fry had arranged for closed coaches to take exiled prisoners to the riverfront. Their families were also permitted to ride with them to the docks. She arranged for each woman to receive a Bible, a pair of reading glasses, a comb, a change of clothing, and a knife and fork. "Let them eat with dignity instead of like animals," she insisted.

For twenty-two years, Elizabeth Fry and her Ladies Committee went on board every convict ship bound for New South Wales. They organized schools for children. They provided work materials to keep hands busy during the voyage. And they set up rules of conduct between prisoners and sailors.

Some Londoners sneered and said, "Why bother? These are just criminals!" But Elizabeth remembered the words of Romans 5:8: "God demonstrates his own love for us in this: While we were still sinners, Christ died for us" (NIV). She knew that her Lord had shown mercy toward her while she was still a sinner. How could she do less for these prisoners?

Mercy means showing kindness to those who may not "deserve" it.

FROM GOD'S WORD:

"Those who show mercy to others are happy, because God will show mercy to them" (Matthew 5:7).

LET'S TALK ABOUT IT:

1. In what way was Elizabeth Fry showing mercy to the prisoners who were being exiled?
2. Can you think of a time when you were shown mercy when you didn't really deserve it—by a parent, a teacher, a friend, maybe even a police officer?
3. Does being merciful or receiving mercy mean not having to face the consequences of bad actions or choices? Why or why not? Can you give examples?

FESTO KIVENGERE

Africa's Apostle of Love

Bloody revolutions ripped the East African country of Uganda during the 1970s and 1980s. Especially violent was the brutal dictator, Idi Amin, who killed as many as three hundred thousand of his fellow citizens.

But God never forgets His people, and to help them through this suffering, He prepared an apostle of His love, Festo Kivengere.

Festo was born in 1919 in a beehive-shaped grass hut. He was the grandson of the last king of the Bahororo tribe, a powerful people who had ruled southwest Uganda for nearly two centuries. Festo grew up worshiping spirits and caring for his father's large herd of cattle in the surrounding lion country.

"Long before the missionaries came to Africa," said Festo, "my people knew there was a God. And we wanted Him; we desired Him. We knew He was the Creator, and so we tried to worship Him." But they did not know how, so they worshiped all kinds of spirits.

Then when Festo was about ten, an African missionary came to his village and built a mud-hut church. He invited the young boys to join his morning classes and learn to read. Festo learned quickly and went away to high school and finally college.

But when he came home years later to be a teacher in his village, he no longer believed in God. But God still cared about Festo. A revival had started in East Africa, and people were going everywhere telling others about Jesus. But the most amazing thing was that people were confessing wrong things they had done to one another and trying to make them right.

This shocked Festo. Religious people usually only pointed out other people's sins. It made Festo think, and finally he became a Christian, too.

Confessing sin and becoming brothers and sisters together in Christ became the core of Festo's ministry. In time, Festo Kivengere became the Anglican Bishop of Kigezi and strengthened the church with deep love.

When Idi Amin tried to stamp out all the Christians in his country, the church remained strong even though many believers died. Festo and his wife had to flee the country, but he wrote a book titled *I Love Idi Amin*. He explained, "On the cross, Jesus said, 'Father, forgive them, because they don't know what they are doing.' As evil as Idi Amin was, how can I do less toward him?"

When Amin was finally thrown out of the country, hatred remained between the people. Until he died of leukemia in 1988, Festo did much to help heal the wounds left by the war.

SURRENDER
No Place to Hide

~~~~~~~~~~~~~~~~~~~~~~~~~~~~~~~~~~~~~~~

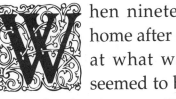hen nineteen-year-old Festo Kivengere returned home after studying to be a teacher, he was surprised at what was happening in his village. Everyone seemed to be talking about Jesus and asking one another for forgiveness. He found this upsetting. *Why don't they keep their religion to themselves?* he complained.

People were singing and repenting in the marketplace, on the road, with their neighbors. There was no escape.

Finally, Festo went to his uncle the chief. His uncle agreed. "This new kind of religion is dangerous. It invades your privacy. You have no place to hide." In the days to come, the chief tried beating those who spoke openly about Jesus. But still, in the evening's quiet, one could hear nothing but Jesus songs floating on the breeze. And in the morning, as the smoke from the cooking fires drifted through the village streets, sounds of the same joyful songs accompanied it.

So the chief arrested twenty Christians and sent them off under guard to the district commissioner. But on the way, the joyful believers converted the guard to Jesus Christ. The guard came back singing like those who had been arrested. What was the chief going to do?

One day, the chief was sitting on his porch with the village elders when a wealthy cattleman came by. His servants were driving eight fine cows before them. All the elders turned to admire the cattle. "Fine-looking cows," called the chief.

"Your Honor," said the rich man, "they are yours. I have brought them back to you."

"What?" said the chief. "I don't recall losing any."

"Well, sir, a couple years ago when I was looking after your cows, I told you there had been a raid by our enemies, and four cows were taken. Do you remember?"

"Yes," said the chief.

"There was no raid," said the cattleman. "I stole them. They had calves, so now there are eight, and I am returning them to you."

"Who discovered this?" asked the chief, frowning.

"Jesus did, sir. You can put me in prison or beat me, but Jesus told me to return them to you, and I am at peace."

The chief was astonished. "If Jesus did that," he said, "who am I to put you in prison. Leave the cattle and go home."

A couple days later, the chief said to Festo, "I must admit, some great power is at work here."

Festo knew that it was Jesus. His twelve-year-old sister and his fourteen-year-old niece had been telling him about Jesus and begging him to go to church. Finally, Festo went, but he was embarrassed when the whole congregation prayed for him. Festo was so angry that he walked out and got drunk.

On his way home, he met a friend who said with great excitement, "Festo, three hours ago Jesus came into my life and forgave my sins. I want you to forgive me, too." And then he named three things for which he wanted forgiveness.

This was too much for Festo. There was no place to hide from this Jesus. When he got home, he knelt by his bed and cried, "God, help me!" And he gave his heart to Jesus.

Surrender is saying yes to Jesus.

FROM GOD'S WORD:

"Here I am! I stand at the door and knock. If you hear my voice and open the door, I will come in and eat with you, and you with me" (Revelation 3:20).

LET'S TALK ABOUT IT:

1. Why did the cattleman return the cows to the chief?
2. Why do you think Festo wanted the Christians to keep their religion to themselves?
3. Why is it good to say yes to Jesus but wrong to say yes to evil things?

REPENTANCE
A Language Anyone Can Understand

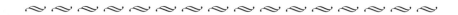

s Festo Kivengere walked up the dusty path to his stepfather's house, he could see a scowl on the old man's face. "What do you want?" snarled the man from where he sat.

For years, Festo had hated the old man and had refused to talk to him. But he knew that must change.

In Festo's village, many things had changed because of the Gospel. A customer surprised the Muslim shopkeeper when he came in and said, "Here are two hundred shillings. I cheated you out of this money. But Jesus has changed my life and wants me to give it back. Please forgive me."

Another Christian went to a government official and said, "Here is a cow to pay my back taxes. I have cheated the government for years, but now I want to make it right."

Another said, "Here, sir, when I worked on the road crew last year, I stole this shovel. Please take it back."

"But why do you bring it back?" asked the road boss.

"I was arrested, sir."

"By whom?"

"By Jesus. He changed my life."

Even Festo's uncle, the old chief, finally gave his life to Jesus. Afterward, he paid back thousands of shillings and many head of cattle to the people he had falsely fined.

Festo also had some things that needed changing. And one of them was his relationship with his stepfather.

When he was ten years old, his father had died of tuberculosis, and his mother had married this man. But he proved to be cruel and often beat Festo's mother. Finally, Festo had to help her and the children move out and live on their own. Not long after that, Festo's mother died, and he had to see to the care of the children himself. Those experiences created great hatred in Festo's heart.

Then one day as Festo prayed, God told him to go and forgive the man. "But I didn't do anything," protested Festo. "He started it all. Besides, he's not a Christian and hasn't repented for beating my mother and ruining our lives."

"Nevertheless," said God, "all broken relationships break my heart. Go and do your part to mend it." Knowing God's heart was broken humbled Festo and made him sad.

Now he stood anxiously on the dusty path wondering what would happen. "Stepfather," he said carefully, "for years I have hated you. But Jesus has taken that hate away."

The old man squinted his eyes, uncertain whether to believe Festo. Finally, he admitted, "Yes, well, I always knew you hated me."

"You knew only a little. I came to tell you the whole story and say that it is over. Please forgive me."

The old man waved Festo closer, and together they sat and talked. An hour later, the man arose, put his arms around Festo, and forgave him. Festo was overcome. He never expected such a reaction, but he later wrote, "Love is a language anyone can understand. The barrier was gone, and we became friends. Now our homes are open to each other."

Repentance is letting your heart be broken over the things in your life that break God's heart.

FROM GOD'S WORD:

[God] says, "I live in a high and holy place, but I also live with those who are sad and humble. I give new life to those who are humble and to those whose hearts are broken" (Isaiah 57:15b).

LET'S TALK ABOUT IT:

1. Why did Festo hate his stepfather?
2. What made Festo's stepfather forgive him?
3. Is there anything in your life that makes God sad?

LOVE
"I Love Idi Amin"

~~~~~~

One bishop's death this week is enough for us," said the frightened believers in the town of Kabale. "Remember Peter! With the help of God's angel, he escaped Herod. So go. Go now!" they urged Festo. "You can help us more from outside the country if you are alive than if you die here."

So Bishop Festo Kivengere and his wife, Mera, didn't even return to their house to get their clothes. They left everything and drove toward the mountains, expecting each moment to meet Idi Amin's soldiers at a road block.

Things had gone from bad to worse in the recent weeks. Amin was killing everyone he thought might be against him. Tens of thousands had already died. Several days before, Amin's soldiers had broken into the home of Festo's friend Archbishop Janani Luwum at 1:30 in the morning and taken him away. Then word came that he had been killed—and Festo was next on Amin's hit list.

But these frightening events did not stop Festo from preaching the Gospel. He said, "Living in danger, when the Lord Jesus is the focus of your life, can be freeing. For one thing, you no longer worry about your safety because you have none. It's all in the Lord's hands."

But it did seem wise to escape if that was possible. Idi Amin's men had already been to his house three times that day looking for Festo. And they had captured and tortured one of his ministers, trying to get the man to tell where Festo was.

As Festo and his wife fled through the night, their Land Rover was stopped by someone standing in the middle of the road. "Go through the forest," the stranger urged. "There's a roadblock up ahead with soldiers waiting to catch you." So they turned off the road and nearly drove off a cliff in the dark before they got back on the road beyond the roadblock. Finally, they arrived at the end of the road and had to continue the last five miles up the mountain by foot. Nine thousand feet up, they reached the border and safety just as the sun rose.

It was easy to hate such an evil man as Idi Amin for causing such suffering and forcing them to leave their home.

But later, as Festo prayed, God said to him, "Can you forgive Amin?"

"No, Lord."

"Suppose he had been one of those soldiers who nailed me to the cross. Do you think I could have prayed, 'Father, forgive them, all except Idi Amin?' "

"No, Master," admitted Festo in prayer. "You would have forgiven even him."

"Then you must do the same, my son."

Some time later, Festo wrote a powerful book, *I Love Idi Amin*. In it he describes the power of love to forgive even the most evil enemy.

Love means forgiving even those who don't deserve to be forgiven.

FROM GOD'S WORD:
"If you love only the people who love you, what praise should you get? Even sinners love the people who love them. . . . But love your enemies, do good to them. . . . Then you will have a great reward" (Luke 6:32, 35a).

LET'S TALK ABOUT IT:
1. Why did Festo and Mera flee Uganda?
2. What caused Festo to realize that he needed to forgive and even love Idi Amin?
3. Describe a time when you acted in love toward someone who had been mean to you.

ERIC LIDDELL

Olympic Champion and
Missionary to China

Eric Liddell was born in China in 1902 to Scottish missionary parents. At age five, he and his older brother, Robbie, returned to the British Isles to go to school in London. The two boys missed their parents and younger sister very much, but seemed to thrive in the boarding school for "sons of missionaries" (later renamed Eltham College).

It soon became apparent that the Liddell brothers were natural athletes. They played rugby and cricket and ran all sorts of track events: cross country, high jump, long jump, 100 yards, hurdles, and quarter mile. But running was Eric's favorite sport, and by the time he entered the university, people were starting to sit up and take notice of his amazing speed.

Eric and Robbie only saw their mother, sister, and baby brother every five years—and it was twelve years before they saw their father again. But when Mary and James Liddell did come home on furlough, they were able to spend one to two years with their growing sons before heading back to China again. The separation of the family was painful to both parents and children. Even though James and Mary were proud of the medals their second son was winning, they sometimes worried whether sports or God would take first place in Eric's heart.

In 1924, at the age of twenty-two, Eric became Britain's hope to win a gold medal at the Paris Olympics. But when the time came, Eric refused to run in his best events—the 100- and 220-meter races—because they were scheduled for Sunday. He was criticized in the press, but criticism turned to admiration when he ran—*and* won, setting a world record for—the 400 meter, a race he had barely trained for.

Scotland and the world had a new sports hero! So everyone was surprised when Eric announced that he was planning to return to China, the land of his birth, as a missionary teacher. And it was in China that he died of a brain tumor at the young age of forty-three while in a communist prison camp for foreigners just months before World War II ended. Besides a wife and three daughters, he left a legacy of simple faith, humility, and sacrificial service to the One who was always the center of his life: Jesus Christ.

PERSEVERANCE
The Impossible Run

spectator in the stadium at Stoke-on-Trent, England, poked his neighbor in the ribs. "Hey, look at that Scottish fellow shaking hands with his rivals—did you ever see such a thing?"

Sure enough, Eric Liddell was going up and down the line of other runners from England, Scotland, and Ireland, shaking hands and saying, "Best wishes for your success." Then he took the place he'd drawn for the quarter-mile race: the inside track starting at the bend.

The year was 1923, and Eric Liddell was a student at Edinburgh University studying science. But a friend, knowing Eric had been outstanding at sports in boarding school, talked him into trying out for the university's athletic events. Now people were saying he had a good chance to represent Britain at the Olympics in 1924.

The starting pistol cracked, and Eric got a good start—for about three strides. Then, suddenly, a runner named Gillies tripped and stumbled against Eric, pushing him off the track onto the grass. Sure that he'd been disqualified, Eric stopped, disappointment welling up in his throat.

But a motion caught his eye. The officials were waving him on! He wasn't disqualified after all. A quick look at the track showed Eric that the runners were a good twenty yards ahead already. Still, almost without thinking, Eric leaped onto the track, his legs pumping furiously.

"What's he think he's doing?" exclaimed the onlooker in the stands. "No one can make up such a distance!"

"Look how he runs," laughed the man's companion. "Head back, arms whipping around—he looks like a swimming circus pony!"

It was true. Eric's running style did look awkward. His head was thrown back, his hands stabbed the air, his knees pumped high like pistons. But to the spectators' surprise, Eric inched past several of the runners and was in fourth place as they turned into the home stretch.

Gillies, the runner who had stumbled, had recovered quickly and was now in first place. And it was obvious to everyone that Eric Liddell's stubborn run had pushed him to the verge of collapse. Still, on he ran, gasping for breath, his legs pumping even higher, harder. In the last few seconds of the race, Eric passed the third-place runner . . . then the second-place man . . . and in a last heroic push, he surged past Gillies and won the race by two yards.

The people in the stands erupted like a volcano, loud cheers filling the stadium. After breaking the finish line tape, Eric fell to the ground, completely winded, his muscles shaking like jelly. A stretcher was called, and Eric was carted off the track to the thunderous cheers of the excited fans, who had never seen such raw determination.

"How did you manage to win such an impossible race?" quizzed a newspaper reporter.

Eric managed a weak grin. "The first half I ran as fast as I could. The second half I ran faster with God's help."

*Perseverance is finishing a task even when
it looks impossible.*

FROM GOD'S WORD:
Jesus looked at them and said, "With man this is impossible, but with God all things are possible" (Matthew 19:26, NIV).

LET'S TALK ABOUT IT:
1. Why do you think Eric ran the race, even though it looked impossible to catch up?
2. What if Eric had not won first place, but came in second or third or fourth? What would you think of his race then?
3. Are you facing a task that seems impossible? What do you think you could do with God's help?

INTEGRITY
"I Can't Run"

ey, Liddell!" yelled one of Eric's Olympic teammates. "The schedule just arrived!"

The team representing Britain—from Scotland, Ireland, England, and Wales—had been eagerly waiting for the 1924 Olympic timetable to see what days and times their sporting events had been scheduled. July was just around the corner, and soon the team would be heading for Paris.

"Two seconds! Your time's up," Eric joked, grabbing the timetable. He eagerly ran his finger down each day's events, looking for the 100-meter race, his best event. Suddenly, the color drained out of his face, and he looked up at his teammates.

"I can't run," he said quietly.

"What?! Can't run? What are you talking about?"

"They've scheduled the first heats for the 100 meter on Sunday."

"So? What's the problem?"

Eric took a deep breath. "I don't run on Sundays. Sunday is for worshiping God, not sports. At least for me."

His teammates just stared, but no one laughed at him. They

respected Eric Liddell too much for that. Even the British officials, though dismayed by the news, quickly tried to get the schedule changed—without any luck.

But when the news got out that Britain's brightest hope for winning a gold medal in the 100-meter race *for the first time ever* was refusing to run, others were not so kind.

"Why can't he run on Sunday and just dedicate the race to God?" some grumbled.

"He's a traitor to his country, that's what he is," others said darkly. "What kind of man would refuse to run for Britain, just because the chosen day doesn't suit him?"

Newspapers scolded him, and people wondered why he was making such a fuss. But Eric Liddell wasn't making a fuss. He was just sticking to a commitment he'd made long ago—a promise to honor Sunday as the Lord's day, a day of rest from work and sports.

Still, Eric was part of Britain's Olympic team, so he began training for the 400-meter race, which was not scheduled for Sunday. Unfortunately, it was not his strongest event. When the team arrived in Paris, newspapers were still criticizing his decision to not run in the 100. On Saturday, Eric marched with his other British teammates, dressed in their cream-colored pants, blue blazers, and white straw hats, in the opening ceremonies. But on Sunday, when the qualifying heats were run, Eric was speaking at a Scots Kirk (Scottish church) in Paris about his commitment to Christ.

On Thursday and Friday, Eric qualified in the initial races and the semi-final for the 400 meter, though his times were nothing special. Just before the final race, a trainer who deeply respected Eric handed him a note that said, "In the old book [the Bible] it says, 'He that honors me I will honor.' Wishing you the best of success always."

Eric shook hands with his rivals and lined up on the track for the final race. The pistol cracked . . . and when the race was over, Eric Liddell had not only won the 400 meter but had set a new world record of 47.6 seconds!

The crowd roared. No one had expected a 100-meter man to run such a race. Criticism turned to admiration. Britain and the world had a new hero—and new respect for a man who lived by what he believed.

Integrity is making choices that honor what you believe, even when people misunderstand you.

FROM GOD'S WORD:

"You must choose for yourselves today whom you will serve. . . . As for me and my family, we will serve the LORD" (Joshua 24:15).

LET'S TALK ABOUT IT:

1. What do you think about Eric Liddell's decision not to run in the Olympics on a Sunday? Would you have made the same choice? Why or why not?
2. Name someone you know who has integrity.
3. In what ways are you faced with choices between what others expect of you and what you believe?

SPORTSMANSHIP
The Flying Scotsman

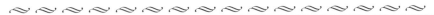

In the 1920s, when Eric Liddell was racing for Scotland, there were no starting blocks at the starting line for runners. Instead they dug a hole in the dirt with the toe of their shoes to help push off. Always full of good ideas, Eric kept a small trowel handy to dig the holes for his toes. Instead of keeping this advantage to himself, however, he would pass the trowel down the line to his rivals, so they could dig holes for their toes, too.

It was just the kind of man he was.

A few weeks before the 1924 Olympics, Eric ran in a Scottish intervarsity race. The day was cool, and a stiff breeze was blowing. Eric noticed one of his competitors sitting beside the track in only a tank top and shorts, shivering. Taking off his blue uniform blazer, he draped it around the other student's shoulders and said kindly, "You must take care not to catch cold."

Just before an international competition, Eric noticed a black runner standing off by himself while the other runners laughed and talked with one another. Leaving the group, Eric went over and drew the loner into a friendly talk.

One day, as Eric took his place on the inside track—the best position—for a 440-yard race, he saw that the man who had drawn the outside track was not a strong runner. At that time, there was no staggering to make up for the curves, so the outside man had to run farther to win. Going over to the other runner, Eric asked if he could change places. "I always feel happier on the outside," he grinned.

Eric's courtesy to others even had a humorous side. When he went back to China as a missionary teacher, he continued to run races. To get to one event, he had to travel by ferry across the river from the city of Tientsin. The last ferry back left at 3:00. To Eric's dismay, he discovered that his race was at 2:30—leaving only half an hour to get to the ferry. So he called a taxi and asked the driver to wait with his motor running at the stadium gate. At 2:30 Eric ran his race—and won. But as he broke the tape at the finish line, he just kept on running for the gate! At that moment, the band struck up "God Save the King," the national anthem of the winner. Eric screeched to a halt and stood with the crowd in respectful silence. As the last note faded, off he dashed again . . . only to be brought to another halt as the band struck up "La Marseillaise" in honor of the Frenchman who came in second.

Finally, he was in the taxi, which sped through the streets to the dock—only to arrive as the ferry was pulling away. Still in his running clothes, Eric sprinted along the dock, took a flying long jump over the fifteen-foot stretch of water, and landed in a heap on the deck. When the story got around of this amazing feat, Eric Liddell became known as "The Flying Scotsman."

Even though Eric was an Olympic champion, he never forgot that there were others who ran hard, ran fast, and ran well. Remembering his teammates and rivals who did not come in first, he said respectfully, "In the dust of defeat as well as in the laurels of victory, there is a glory to be found if one has done his best."

Sportsmanship is showing respect to others, even rivals in a game or competition.

FROM GOD'S WORD:
When you do things, do not let selfishness or pride be your guide. Instead, be humble and give more honor to others than to yourselves (Philippians 2:3).

LET'S TALK ABOUT IT:
1. How do you think Eric Liddell's Christian faith affected his sportsmanship?
2. To have a winner, there must also be losers. What was Eric's attitude toward "losers"?
3. In what ways does Eric Liddell's example encourage you to show better sportsmanship?

WATCHMAN NEE

Leader of the Chinese House Church Movement

The Chinese mother lay awake in the night listening to the night watchman make his rounds. Lin Huo-ping desperately wanted a baby boy. The Ni family already had two girls, and in Chinese culture, a family was disgraced if they had no male heirs. "Oh, God," she prayed, "I will give this baby back to serve you, if you will only give me a son."

When *Ni Shu-tsu* ("He who proclaims his ancestor's merits") was born on November 4, 1903, in Swatow, China, there was a big celebration. (He was later joined by four younger brothers and two more sisters.) True to her word, Huo-ping dedicated this child to God's service. As the child grew into a young man, he wanted a name that reflected his mission in life: preaching the Word of God and sharing God's love with his people.

Lin Huo-ping told her son about the night she lay awake listening to the watchman and the promise she had made God. "How about Ni To-sheng?" she suggested. "To-sheng means 'the watchman.' " And that is how Watchman Nee got his name.

Watchman Nee was greatly influenced by Christian missionaries, especially Margaret Barber, an Englishwoman. But he was troubled that the foreign missions were divided by denominations—Presbyterian, Christian Missionary Alliance, and so forth. Watchman thought all Christians in each city should come together as one true, local church under Jesus Christ. Because of his teaching, many house churches were begun, called "Church Assemblies," completely free of foreign connections. But even though Watchman's desire was oneness in the church, many who were drawn to these "assemblies" left other churches—and so there were hard feelings and criticism. This movement, however, gave rise to many of the Chinese house churches. These churches continued a faithful Christian witness even after the Communists expelled all foreigners from the country.

In 1952, Watchman Nee was arrested by the Communists. He was charged as a "counter-revolutionary" and with corrupting the minds of young people. He remained in prison until his death in 1972. But many of his writings, such as *The Normal Christian Life* and *Sit, Walk, Stand*, still inspire Christians all over the world.

TRUST
Only Tell God

~~~~~~

Are you sure God wants you to quit school to preach the Gospel?" the English missionary asked the young Chinese man who had come to see her.

Watchman Nee nodded. Since he had given his life to Jesus, the way he looked at life had changed. The things he was studying at the university no longer interested him. He had only one passion: to preach the Word of God. "But if I don't go to school, I lose my college scholarship," he admitted to his friend. "I don't know how I will take care of myself."

Miss Barber smiled. "I worried about money, too, when I first became a missionary. But a dear Christian friend told me, 'If God sends you, He must be responsible.' And God has met every need."

Watchman carried Miss Barber's words in his heart. *If it's God's responsibility to care for me,* Watchman told himself, *then I don't need to tell other people about my needs. God knows what they are.*

As Watchman Nee was preaching in his hometown of Foochow, he got a letter from a former classmate, also a Christian.

"Please come to Chien-O to preach at some evangelistic meetings," said the letter.

Watchman felt his heart stir. He very much wanted to go. But Chien-O was one hundred fifty miles upriver, and the fare by motor boat was eighty dollars! Watchman counted his money: thirty dollars. "But if God is sending me, then God is responsible," he reminded himself.

The day before he was to leave on his trip, Watchman heard about a friend who badly needed money. God seemed to be telling him to help his friend. Watchman gulped. Could he trust God to take care of him if he shared his money with someone else? His faith felt shaky, but he sent twenty dollars to his friend.

As he headed toward the river dock the next day, Watchman had only ten dollars in his pocket. "Oh, Lord," he prayed, "I'm not asking you for money. Only a way to get to Chien-O."

At the dock, the owner of a small boat yelled at him, "Are you going to Yen-ping or Chien-O?"

"Chien-O," Watchman yelled back.

"I'll take you then—only seven dollars," said the man, taking Watchman's bags and putting them on his boat. In amazement, Watchman learned that someone else had hired this boat to take some cargo to Chien-O, but the boatman still had room for one passenger.

Watchman Nee preached for two weeks in Chien-O with only one dollar and twenty cents in his pocket. As he got ready to leave, one of the English missionaries said, "You have helped us so much. Can we help you with your expenses?"

With only a few coins in his pocket, Watchman had no idea how he was going to get home. But he said, "There is no need. All is fully taken care of."

As he walked back to the dock, however, he felt anxious and

worried. "Oh, God," he prayed, "You got me here. You'll have to get me back!"

Just then a messenger caught up to him with a note and some money. It was from the grateful missionary. "Even though you have someone to pay your fare," the note said, "please accept this gift and let me play a small part."

Now Watchman knew this was how God was meeting his need. And there was the same boat, willing to take him back to Foochow for only seven dollars!

Trust in God includes recognizing when God is working through others.

FROM GOD'S WORD:
What you have can help others who are in need. Then later, when they have plenty, they can help you when you are in need (2 Corinthians 8:14).

LET'S TALK ABOUT IT:
1. Why did Watchman give twenty dollars away when he needed money for his own fare?
2. Why did Watchman accept the missionary's gift the second time it was offered?
3. What do you think about Watchman Nee's rule of telling only God what he needed?

FAITH
It Rained on Their Parade

~~~~~~

The holiday celebrations in the Chinese village of Mei-hua were in full swing. Families made ceremonial visits and burned incense to their ancestors. Men laughed and gambled. Huge feasts were prepared, and offerings were made to the household gods. At night, fireworks lit up the sky.

Watchman Nee and six other young preachers tried to share the Gospel with the noisy holiday crowds. They spread out around the town and preached on the street corners. A few villagers stopped to listen, but most people just hurried by. Finally on the ninth day, Li Kuo-ching, the youngest preacher and a new believer himself, cried in frustration to the crowd, "What's wrong? Why won't you believe?"

A villager shrugged. "Why should we? We have our own god, Ta-wang [Great King]. His feast day is two days away. And for 286 years, Ta-wang has sent sunshine for his feast day without fail. He's very dependable."

"Then I promise you," cried Li, "our God, who is the true God, will make it rain on Ta-wang's feast day."

Immediately, the villagers were interested. It was like a game, a contest. "Agreed!" they cried. "If it rains on Ta-wang's feast day, then your Jesus is indeed God. We will be ready to hear about Him."

The news of Li's challenge spread rapidly all over the village. When Watchman Nee heard it, he was horrified. Li was young and inexperienced. He had put God's honor to the test in a reckless way. What if God did not choose to make it rain on the feast day? If it did not rain, no one would listen to them preach about Jesus in the future.

But that night as the young men prayed, Watchman sensed God speaking to him: *"Where is the God of Elijah?"* In the Bible, Watchman remembered, the prophet Elijah had challenged the priests of Baal to a similar contest. Both Elijah and the pagan priests had built altars and sacrificed an animal. Elijah even poured buckets of water over his sacrifice. But only Elijah's God, the one true God, had sent fire to burn up the sacrifice.

Now all seven young men got excited. They felt sure that the God of Elijah whom they preached would send rain on Ta-wang's feast day.

When the little band of preachers woke up on the feast day of Ta-wang, sunshine streamed through the windows. Watchman was tempted to pray, "Oh, Lord, please make it rain!" but the still, small voice just said, *"Where is the God of Elijah?"* So instead of begging God, the young men just settled down to eat their breakfast. As they bowed their heads to thank God for the food, rain pattered on the window tiles. As they finished their first bowl of rice, it was coming down in a steady shower. As they began on their second bowl of rice, the rain had become a downpour.

At the first sign of rain, some of the villagers said, "Jesus is God! There is no more Ta-wang!" But Ta-wang's worshipers insisted on carrying their idol in a parade anyway. Surely their god would stop the rain on his feast day! But by this time the streets were flooded, and the parade marchers stumbled and slipped. Down went the idol, cracking its jaw and left arm as it fell.

By now, the whole village was eager to listen to the Gospel. Satan's power had been broken when the idol fell.

Faith is knowing that our God is the one true God.

FROM GOD'S WORD:
The LORD is the only true God. He is the only living God, the King forever (Jeremiah 10:10).

LET'S TALK ABOUT IT:
1. Why was Watchman Nee upset when he first heard about Li's challenge to the pagan god? What changed his attitude?
2. Why didn't the preachers beg God to send rain?
3. What is the difference between "testing" God and "believing" (having faith) in God's power?

PRAYER

Victory in War?

~~~~~~~~~~~~~~~~~~~~~~~~~~~~~~~~~~~

The tall, slender man in the shabby blue gown and rumpled felt hat walked through the ghostly streets of Shanghai, his heart aching. The world was at war in 1940, and China was no exception. The Japanese had invaded China in 1937 and were coming closer, taking city after city. In Shanghai, once a bustling, rich city, people did not go outside unless they had to. But Watchman Nee had a pastor's heart, and every day he visited the homes of his fellow Christians to encourage them, pray with them, and see if there was a need that should be met.

"Oh, Pastor Nee," exclaimed one couple during a visit. "We are praising God that our business has not been harmed and we are not suffering like so many are."

Something is wrong, Watchman thought. *How can we praise God that we are not suffering when so many around us are hurting? Isn't God's heart broken? Shouldn't our hearts be broken for those who suffer?*

In another home, a group of believers gathered to pray that God would stop Japan and give China a war victory. This made Watchman Nee think hard. The whole world was at war . . . but weren't there also Christians in Japan? in Germany? in America? in Britain? Were they all praying for themselves and against their enemies? Surely Christians must pray during this crisis! But how should Christians pray during wartime?

Gathering the local believers together, Watchman said, "I want to talk to you, not as Chinese people, but as men and women in Christ." He then gave a spiritual history lesson on God's use of government in the lives of His people—beginning with the kings of Persia who captured the Hebrews when they disobeyed God, up to the present. "God is not interested in the future of a particular nation," Watchman said gravely, "but in the obedience of His people all over the world."

The people shifted uneasily on the hard benches. What was Pastor Nee trying to say?

"In this time of crisis," Watchman went on, "we must not only pray, but we must know *how* to pray. When we pray, it must be possible for British and German, for Chinese and Japanese Christians to kneel and pray together, and all to say 'Amen' to what is asked. If not, there is something wrong with our prayer."

The people looked sideways at one another. Could they kneel together with Japanese—even Japanese *Christians*—and pray together? Wasn't Japan's invading China just plain *wrong*?

As if reading their minds, Watchman Nee said, "We may tell God what we see wrong with the attitude Japan has toward Him—but we must also confess to God that in China many Christians and missionaries have too much relationship with the government."

"What, then, shall we pray?" the people cried.

"The Church must stand above national questions and say, 'Father, we ask neither for a Chinese nor a Japanese victory—but for whatever will bring glory to your Son, Jesus Christ.'" Watchman paused and looked around the room at the faces of those who, like him, loved Jesus Christ more than life itself. "If the whole Church around the world prayed such a prayer, the war could soon be settled God's way. But let it begin with us. . . ."

Prayer is praying for the glory of God's kingdom on earth, not for the glory of ourselves or our nation.

FROM GOD'S WORD:

"So when you pray, you should pray like this: 'Our Father . . . May your kingdom come and what you want be done, here on earth as it is in heaven'" (Matthew 6:9–10).

LET'S TALK ABOUT IT:

1. Why was Watchman Nee uncomfortable praying for a Chinese victory over Japan?
2. How does what Watchman Nee said about prayer fit together with how Jesus said to pray in The Lord's Prayer (Matthew 6)?
3. Talk about how your family should pray for your country and the world during times of trouble and crisis.

JOHN NEWTON

———————— ❧ ————————

The Slave Trader Who
Found Grace

When John Newton's kind mother died before his seventh birthday, he felt very alone. Since his birth in London in 1725, she had raised him mostly by herself because his sea captain father was often away on long trips.

But then life changed for John. Even though his father re-married, John's stepmother did not want him around and sent him off to boarding school.

When he was eleven, his father took him to sea. *Maybe now he will spend time with me*, hoped John, but his father was too busy.

Later, John was drafted into the British Royal Navy. He tried to escape but was caught and severely whipped. When his ship put into port near north Africa to make repairs, John arranged to trade himself for a skilled carpenter from another ship. He was glad to get out of the navy.

Thinking that life was treating him badly, John decided to treat others the same. He made life worse for himself by refusing to obey orders. Finally, he got work with a slave trader along the African coast. But then he himself was made a slave!

His father finally arranged his rescue, but the hard things John had experienced did not teach him to be kind to others. By the age of twenty-two, he became the captain of his own slave ship.

Then one day, his ship was caught in a violent storm and nearly sank. When all seemed lost, John remembered the Lord his mother had told him about. He repented of his sins, and God saved him.

John Newton became a minister, worked to end slavery, and wrote many songs. His most famous hymn tells his own story: "Amazing grace! how sweet the sound that saved a wretch like me!"

DESTINY
Saved for a Purpose

One day, young John Newton went horseback riding with some of his friends. Suddenly, a large bird flew up out of the grass near the trail with such a whir of its wings that it scared John's horse. The horse reared up and threw John off. He landed on his back on the ground. The thud knocked the breath out of him.

As he gasped for air, he noticed that he had landed just inches from some sharp stakes that could have killed him if he had hit them. Someone had chopped down a hedgerow along the trail. The dried, pointed stumps of the tough little trees created a bed of sharpened spikes each a foot long. If he had landed on them, they would have pierced straight through him.

His friends said he was just lucky, but John remembered his mother's words about God's love—that God loved him and had a purpose for his life.

But John soon forgot this lesson and went on with his selfish life without any thought of how God might want him to live.

A couple years later, John and some other boys decided to row a little boat out into the river to see a big warship that was anchored there. They planned their adventure for the next morning, but being lazy, John overslept and arrived at the river late.

The other boys had grown tired of waiting for John and left without him. They were already out in the boat laughing and yelling and having a great time. John yelled and screamed for them to come back and get him, but they only called insults at him. "See you later, John Boy," they cried. "Why don't you fix us something nice to eat for when we get back."

John was so angry that he stomped back and forth along the bank calling them names. If he'd known how to swim, he would have dived in and headed after them.

But as he watched, a couple of the boys stood up in the boat, and the boat tipped over. All kinds of splashing followed as the boys scrambled for safety. Finally, a boat was launched from the warship to rescue them before they drifted downriver and out to sea.

But by then, John's best friend had drowned.

In his grief over the death of his friend, John realized that if he had been in the boat, he would have drowned, too, because he couldn't swim. God had saved him again! But still John paid no attention.

Years later when he was made a slave in Africa, he was treated so badly that he almost died. But again, just in time, he was rescued. Why was God always saving him? John still didn't take time to think about the question.

Finally, when John became a ship's captain, a terrible storm nearly sank his ship. This time, John remembered God and prayed for help. When God saved the ship, John Newton finally realized that God loved him and had a purpose for his life.

*Discovering your destiny—what God has planned
for you—begins by believing that God loves you
and has a special purpose for your life.*

FROM GOD'S WORD:

Now this is what the LORD says. . . . "Don't be afraid,
because I have saved you. I have called you by
name, and you are mine" (Isaiah 43:1).

LET'S TALK ABOUT IT:

1. How did God save John Newton's life?
2. Why didn't John recognize that God had a
   purpose for his life?
3. Tell about a time that God saved your life or ask
   an adult to tell about a time when he or she could
   have died. Thank God for loving you and having
   a purpose for your life.

PERSEVERANCE
The Minister No One Wanted

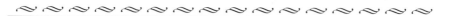

fter John Newton retired from being a sea captain, he worked as a trade inspector. During this time, he and his wife, Mary, had many friends over to their home for Sunday evening prayer meetings. These were joyful times of singing and telling one another what God had done for them.

Often, people asked John to tell how God rescued him. But when John was asked to stand up in church and tell the same story, he froze with fear. The minister asked him to try a second time the next week. Again, John felt afraid, but the fear was not as bad. The third time, he got through the whole thing without giving up. After that, he was asked to speak so often that his friends suggested he become a minister.

Could this be the purpose for which God had repeatedly saved his life? The more John prayed about it, the more interested he became. When a minister from another town heard of his interest, he invited John to take over a small chapel. All he needed were letters from three ministers who recommended him and the bishop's appointment.

The letters of recommendation were easy to get, but the bishop was not so certain. He liked John, but since John had no formal training, he wouldn't appoint him to be a minister.

John tried several other places and was always turned down. At last, he became so discouraged and sad that he almost gave up. But when the Earl of Dartmouth heard of John's interest, he asked John to pastor the church in the town of Olney. *Certainly with the earl's support I can get an appointment*, thought John. This time, John went to the Archbishop of York, who was holding examinations in London to appoint new ministers. But when the clerk learned that John had been refused by other bishops, he wouldn't even let John in to speak to the archbishop.

John ran a mile and a half across town to the earl's home and told him what had happened. The earl wrote him a note addressed to the archbishop and put his official seal on it. John ran back across town and presented it to the clerk. The clerk couldn't refuse that. But to John's dismay, the archbishop would not appoint him.

The archbishop said he was sorry that he couldn't help. He liked John but didn't feel he could take the responsibility of overseeing his ministry. He did, however, have one more suggestion. "Try the Bishop of Lincoln."

Without much hope, John visited the bishop, and after a long examination of John's understanding of the Bible and his desire to become a minister, he agreed to appoint him.

John and Mary were delighted. With a joyous send-off from their friends, they moved to Olney. There, John's sermons were so popular that the church had to be enlarged.

But his greatest joy came as he and Mary got to know William and Mary Cowper. The Cowpers moved in next door to the Newtons, and they became best friends. William was a poet, and by then John had discovered that he liked writing songs. Together, the two men had song-writing contests. It was during this period that Newton wrote such famous songs as "Amazing Grace," "How Sweet the Name of Jesus Sounds," "Glorious Things of Thee Are Spoken," and many others.

Perseverance means not giving up even when everything seems to be going wrong.

FROM GOD'S WORD:
You must hold on, so you can do what God wants and receive what he has promised (Hebrews 10:36).

LET'S TALK ABOUT IT:
1. What happened the first time John Newton tried to speak in church? the second time? the third time?
2. What good things came to John because he didn't give up?
3. Tell about a time when you had to try something several times before you were able to do it.

RESTITUTION
The Stranger in the Heavy Coat

s Pastor John Newton greeted the people after church, a stranger in a heavy coat approached him and slipped an envelope into his hand. "Sir," the man whispered, "allow me to give you this. It is very important." And then the man was gone.

How strange, thought Newton. *What could this be?*

Earlier, John Newton had written in a song, "Amazing grace! how sweet the sound that saved a wretch like me!"

Why would a preacher call himself something as awful a name as "wretch"? Possibly he was remembering the misery he had caused as a slave ship captain. The slave trade truly was an evil business. It involved kidnapping Africans from their homes, packing them into ships where many died or went crazy as they crossed the sea, and then selling them into a cruel life of slavery.

After Newton became a Christian, God spoke to him. Even though many people in those days thought slavery was all right, God reminded Newton of the horrible suffering it caused. And the more he thought about it, the more it made him sick. He began to see his own sin the way God saw it—a terrible, ugly thing. It had certainly taken God's "amazing grace" to save someone as wicked as he.

Newton was sorry for his sin and thankful that God had saved him. In his thankfulness, he prayed, "Oh, God, allow me to help in some small way to make things right." But what could he do? He couldn't bring back the captives who had died at sea. He couldn't return the living slaves to their homeland. What could he do?

God's answer came in the form of the stranger in the heavy coat. When Newton opened the envelope the man had given him that cold Sunday morning, he found a letter from William Wilberforce, an important government official. "I feel God has some important plan for my life," Wilberforce wrote. "Will you help me discover it?"

Newton was delighted. Could this be the answer to his prayers? As a government official, Wilberforce might be able to help change the laws and end slavery.

Together, Newton and Wilberforce worked hard. And in 1807, just months before John Newton died, the British government passed a law ending England's role in the slave trade. Wilberforce continued to work to set things right, and in 1825, all the slaves in England were freed.

Restitution does not earn forgiveness. But in thankfulness for being forgiven, we choose to make right the wrong.

FROM GOD'S WORD:

Zacchaeus stood and said to the Lord, "I will give half of my possessions to the poor. And if I have cheated anyone, I will pay back four times more" (Luke 19:8).

LET'S TALK ABOUT IT:

1. Why did John Newton call himself a "wretch"? What do you think that word means?
2. For what did John Newton pray?
3. When you do something wrong, the most important thing is to say you are sorry and ask for forgiveness. But even after the person forgives you, why is it good to try to make it right?

FLORENCE NIGHTINGALE

A Nurse at Heart

Florence Nightingale was born into a wealthy British family on May 12, 1820. She had every privilege available: clothes, parties, lessons, servants, horses . . . but she was bored and frustrated with her life. She wanted to do something useful.

At the age of sixteen, she wrote in her diary: "On Feb. 7, God spoke to me and called me to His service." What service, she didn't know. But as she grew to womanhood, she realized she felt most fulfilled and content when she was caring for the sick in the poor cottages around Embley, the family home.

Yet in the 1840s, nurses had a poor reputation as drunkards, prostitutes, and "maids-of-all-work." "Proper" English women from good families did not work in common hospitals. Florence was thirty-three years old before she persuaded her parents to let her take her first nursing job in a private hospital for "gentlewomen."

When England and France declared war on Russia in 1854, the English government asked Florence Nightingale to take a team of nurses to the Crimea. Conditions in the military hospitals were terrible; many more soldiers died from disease, poor food and water, and neglect than died from enemy wounds.

She discovered that fighting "the army way of doing things" was an uphill battle—but at the end of the Crimean War, Florence Nightingale was a national heroine. Funds were raised to establish the Nightingale School of Nursing in London. Until her death in 1910, she worked tirelessly to change health and medical care in the army for the better. She is now considered the "founder of modern nursing" not only in England, but all over the world.

KINDNESS
Poor Old Cap

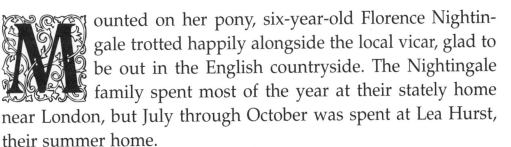

Mounted on her pony, six-year-old Florence Nightingale trotted happily alongside the local vicar, glad to be out in the English countryside. The Nightingale family spent most of the year at their stately home near London, but July through October was spent at Lea Hurst, their summer home.

As they rode down a lane alongside a large, grassy pasture, Florence suddenly pulled her pony to a stop. "Look, pastor, something is wrong," said young Florence, pointing to the snowy sheep dotting the pasture here and there. "All the sheep are scattered. Old Roger, the shepherd, can't collect them himself. Something must be wrong with Cap, his sheep dog."

Sure enough, when the vicar and the little girl found Old Roger, the shepherd shook his head sadly. "Some boys threw rocks at Cap and broke his leg. I'm afraid I'll have to put an end to him."

"Oh no!" cried Florence. "Where is he? We must do something to help him."

The old shepherd pointed to a nearby shed. "But you can't do anything for him, missy. It's better if I put him out of his misery."

Florence kicked her pony into a gallop. A few minutes later, she was sitting beside the injured collie, who was lying on the floor. "Oh, pastor, can't we do something?" she cried as she gently stroked the dog's head.

The vicar knelt down and carefully felt the damaged leg. "I don't think the leg is broken," he mused, "only badly bruised. With some good nursing, he should pull through."

The vicar and young Florence brought hot water and kept the injured leg wrapped in hot cloths. When Old Roger arrived that evening to destroy the dog, Cap wagged his tail and nuzzled his master's hand.

"See? He's perked up already!" Florence cried. "Please let me nurse him—I'll come every day to take care of him."

She was true to her word. Faithfully, she came every day to sit with the dog, soothe the bruises with hot cloths, and give him food and water. When at last Cap was back up on all four legs, she could hardly contain her joy.

Years later, when Florence Nightingale had become widely known all over England for saving the lives of wounded soldiers during the Crimean War, the vicar, now an old man, wrote her a letter:

"I wonder whether you remember how, many years ago, you and I averted the death of Old Roger's sheep dog, Cap? I remember the pleasure that saving the life of a poor dog gave to your young mind. I was delighted to witness it. To me, it wasn't an omen of what you would grow up to be and do—I never dreamed of it!—but it was a sign of the kindness and love spoken of in 1 Corinthians 13 taking root within you."

Kindness is not a feeling of pity, but love put into action.

FROM GOD'S WORD:

Love is patient and kind (1 Corinthians 13:4a).

LET'S TALK ABOUT IT:

1. How do you suppose Old Roger felt when Cap didn't have to be destroyed after all?
2. How did helping the injured dog show what kind of person Florence would grow up to be?
3. How can you turn feelings of pity into "loving kindness"?

PATIENCE
Locked Out

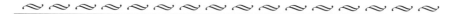

he sharp wind blowing off the Bay of Bosphorus was bitter cold. Florence Nightingale pulled her hooded cloak more tightly around her and trudged through the muddy snow toward the British military hospital. She had been in Turkey only a couple months, trying to improve the way wounded and sick soldiers were cared for during wartime. But many of the medical officers did not listen to her suggestions. Some of them ignored her. A few were even rude.

Still, she did what she could, and one thing she did every day was visit all the patients, giving them a cool drink, a word of comfort, or offering to write a letter for them to a mother or sweetheart.

A young boy about twelve years old huffed alongside her. Robbie was a drummer boy who had lost his hand at the Battle of Alma in the Crimea, where the war was being fought across the Black Sea. No longer able to drum for his regiment, he had named himself "Miss Nightingale's man," often going with her on her rounds, running errands, and doing whatever he could to be helpful to her.

The road to the hospital was frozen into deep ruts, but soon the hospital loomed ahead. "Here we are, Miss Nightingale," the boy said cheerfully, his breath coming out in little puffs in the cold air. He pulled on the big wooden door with his good hand—but the door didn't budge.

Puzzled, Florence stepped forward and tugged on the handle. Then she rattled it hard.

"Is it stuck, Miss Nightingale?" asked the boy.

Florence frowned. "No, not stuck—locked." She shook her head in frustration. The British officers knew she came every day to visit the patients. This was their way of telling her she didn't belong there. But . . . she had a job to do. The British Secretary at War had sent her to the Crimea. She and her nurses were here with his authority.

It was going to take more than a locked door to keep her out.

"Robbie," she said, "run back to the other hospital and get a key, would you? Say I am locked out and will wait here until the door is unlocked."

"But, Miss Nightingale, it's cold! You'll freeze," the boy protested.

"Go," she ordered. "I'll be all right."

The drummer boy stumbled off down the rutted path. Hours went by. Most of the time, Florence stubbornly sat on a nearby bench. When she got too cold, she walked back and forth in front of the locked door. But the winter daylight was already fading when Robbie finally came trudging back with a key.

As Florence turned the key in the lock and pulled open the heavy door, Robbie grumbled, "Ain't you mad, miss? To be treated so rudely—and you a lady at that!"

Florence gave a short laugh. "Oh yes, I get angry at people's foolishness. But, Robbie, when people offend, they offend the Master before they do me."

Patience sometimes means suffering wrong things
that people do, knowing the sin
is really against God.

FROM GOD'S WORD:
The LORD told Samuel, "Listen to whatever the people say to you. They have not rejected you. They have rejected me from being their king" (1 Samuel 8:7).

LET'S TALK ABOUT IT:
1. Why do you think the British army gave Florence Nightingale such a hard time when she just wanted to help?
2. What do you think she meant when she said, "They offend the Master before they do me"?
3. Do you know people who are rude or mean to you? How would remembering that they are really offending God help make you more patient with them?

GENEROSITY
Six Lousy Shirts

~~~~~~~~~~~~~~~~~~~~~~~~~~~~~~~~

Six shirts a month?" cried Florence Nightingale in dismay.

More than a thousand wounded and sick soldiers lined the hallways and wards of the crowded Barracks Hospital. Their uniforms were filthy, covered with dirt, lice, and dried blood. Anxious to get the soldiers into some clean clothes, Florence had asked a medic how many clean shirts were available.

The medic shrugged. "The men are afraid to send their shirts to be washed, for fear they'll be stolen. I think only six shirts were washed and came back last month."

"But—where are the hospital shirts?" Florence demanded. "Most of the men's shirts are nothing but rags and should be burned, not washed! And what about the dirty bedding? Some of these men have infectious diseases!"

Again the medic shook his head helplessly. "Maybe the supply officer has ordered some—maybe not. All I know is that it takes weeks for any supplies to get through all the red tape, and even then it's never enough."

This was not good enough for Florence Nightingale. Red tape, indeed! Didn't the army know that dirt and lice kept the wounded and sick from getting well again?

Taking along one or two helpers, Florence Nightingale marched into the town market. When she returned hours later, she was followed by several Turkish carts, piled high with brand-new shirts.

"Where did these come from?" asked the shocked supply officer.

"I bought them," said Florence as she directed the unloading.

"But . . . but this is very unusual!" sputtered the supply officer.

"Yes, I suppose so," said Florence. "Excuse me, but my nurses and I have work to do." While her nurses went to work bathing the hundreds of wounded and sick men and dressing them in clean clothes, Florence set out on another errand. Using her own money and some that others had given, she rented a nearby house, had boilers installed, and hired soldiers' wives to wash the hospital bedding.

Florence Nightingale rarely spent money on herself. Most of her personal money helped buy food for patients who needed special diets—or more bedpans or soap or warm socks to help the men.

Even her time was spent on others. Whatever needed doing, Florence was willing to do it, whether it was scrubbing floors, bandaging wounds, ripping old, clean sheets into bandages, or comforting a dying patient. Sometimes it was two or three o'clock in the morning before she fell into bed, so tired she could barely move.

A friend who visited Florence Nightingale in Turkey remarked later, "To give less than every ounce of strength would not have been enough for Florence—would not be what God expected of her. For God was the only master she would acknowledge; she was His representative at Scutari; the work she did was His work. In that thought was all the reward, all the pleasure she desired. Her only thought was, 'Thy will be done.' "

Generosity is freely using the gifts God has given you to help others.

FROM GOD'S WORD:
He will make you rich in every way so that you can always give freely (2 Corinthians 9:11a).

LET'S TALK ABOUT IT:
1. Why did Florence spend her own money to do something the British army was supposed to do?
2. What percentage of her time and money did Florence give generously and freely to others?
3. What can you do to be more generous with your money? with your time?

JOHN PERKINS

———— ❦ ————

A Man Hate Couldn't Stop

The Perkins family were sharecroppers like most blacks in Mississippi in the 1930s and 1940s. Some were also bootleggers and gamblers—and unlike most black folks who were afraid to cross "The Man" (white people), "a Perkins ain't afraid to stand up to nobody."

John Perkins was tough, too. He had to be. His mama died in 1930 when he was only seven months old, and his daddy took off, leaving the kids in the care of John's grandmother. John wasn't religious, but he hung around the country church because that was the only place black folks could get together and socialize.

But when his older brother, Clyde, was shot and killed by a white deputy while standing outside a movie theater, the family sent sixteen-year-old John to California for his own safety. It was a chance to start over, away from the open racism of the South, and he knew how to work hard. Soon the school dropout was experiencing a new feeling—success. Eventually, John married his sweetheart from back home, brought her to California, and started a family. This Perkins was going to be somebody!

But God interrupted John's plans. Visiting the church his

young son attended, John accepted Jesus Christ, the living God who changes lives. He began reading the Bible for the first time. Discipled by others, he began speaking and preaching in both black and white churches. And then God told him to go back to Mississippi to help young people like himself who were going nowhere. It wasn't easy to return to the South in the 1960s—and at one point, it nearly cost him his life.

Today, John Perkins is known as a man who puts the Gospel to work. In Mississippi, he began Mendenhall Ministries and Voice of Calvary, ministering to the whole person. In California, his vision for transforming people and communities has taken shape in the Harambee Family Christian Center and the Christian Community Development Association (CCDA), bringing blacks and whites together in partnership for the sake of the Gospel. Now back in Mississippi, John is developing the Reconcilers Fellowship Training Center, which sponsors a variety of conferences for reconciliation and development. Reconcilers Fellowship publishes *Reconcilers* magazine.

WISDOM
One Small Push for Justice

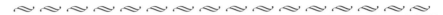

The white farmer looked twelve-year-old John Perkins up and down. "Can you do a man's work? I need help getting this hay in afore it rains."

"Yes, sir!" John said. John's family were share-croppers, and he knew how to work hard. But this was his own chance to earn some pocket money. He wondered how much the man would pay, but he didn't dare ask. The going rate for a day's work in Mississippi in 1942 was a dollar and a half—maybe two.

John threw hay bales into the wagon with all the muscle he could muster. Sweat poured down his back. By the end of the day, the hay had been hauled from the field, stacked, and covered.

Standing in the man's kitchen, John waited expectantly.

"Here's your pay," said the farmer, holding out a couple coins. A dime and a nickel—fifteen cents.

John just stood there. It was so unfair! He knew he'd hate him-self if he took it. But he was afraid not to take it, afraid the man would call him an "uppity nigger" and other white folks would give him a hard time for "not knowing his place."

He took the fifteen cents.

John was angry as he scuffed his way home. Why was the man able to cheat him like that? He realized that the man had the "capital" (the land and the hay) and the "means of production" (the wagon and horses). All John had to offer was his labor. So it was the man with the capital and the means of production who made the money and set the price.

It was John's first lesson in economics, and he didn't forget it. When he was fourteen, he and his cousin Jimmy took a job for a white farmer who was considered fair-minded. The boys agreed to clear a pasture of bushes and undergrowth for a gallon of syrup and a meal per day. It was hard, back-breaking work, and by noon the boys were ready for that hot meal. But when they appeared at the house, the man's mother-in-law handed out a plate of "leavings" (table scraps).

The boys looked at each other. No way could they work all day for a few leavings. They put down their tools and went home.

When the farmer heard what had happened, he came to the boys' house and urged them to come back. He'd make sure they got a square meal if they'd finish the job. The boys agreed. John later said, "It was my first small push for justice."

Determined to use his knowledge of the way the economic "system" worked to better himself, John went to California as a young man and got a job in a new factory. His crew came up with ideas to streamline production, which made more money for the company. Then John helped organize the workers into a union so that the workers could cash in on the increased money the company made. That success felt good!

But then God got hold of John Perkins and changed his life. Eventually, he left a good job and a nice home in California to return to Mississippi to share the Gospel, bringing spiritual hope to the poor. He also used what he knew about economics not for his own benefit, but to bring economic hope to poor communities.

Wisdom is knowledge that is used in God's way.

FROM GOD'S WORD:
Are there those among you who are truly wise and understanding? Then they should show it by living right and doing good things with a gentleness that comes from wisdom (James 3:13).

LET'S TALK ABOUT IT:
1. Why didn't twelve-year-old John want to take his fifteen-cent pay?
2. How did John make what he learned about "economics" work for him? work for God?
3. Talk about other kinds of human knowledge that can become spiritual wisdom.

FORGIVENESS
Beaten in the Brandon Jail

~~~~~~~~~~~~~~~~~~~~~~~~~~~~

The voice on the telephone was crying. "The highway police arrested Doug and the students and took them to the Brandon jail!"

Rev. John Perkins put the receiver down and looked at his wife, Vera Mae. "I've got to go to Brandon and do something," he said quietly. "We've got to take a stand against these false arrests and beatings in jail."

Perkins had already been in jail once—just before Christmas, when he and other folks from Voice of Calvary Ministries in Mendenhall, Mississippi, went to see a black teenager who'd been put in jail. They'd heard he'd been beaten. The whole group had been "arrested"—including children—but they were never told what the charges were. Vera Mae and others from the community went to the jail, but they felt helpless and didn't know what to do. In 1969, black folks in Mississippi felt powerless against the whites who controlled everything.

That's when John Perkins got the idea for a boycott in Mendenhall. Whites owned everything—but they depended on black folks to buy from their stores. If blacks refused to buy, maybe the white folks would listen to what blacks wanted: justice, fairness, and jobs.

The boycott started at Christmas and continued for several weeks. It got the attention of the store owners all right. It also made a lot of the whites mad.

Now it was February and Doug, a white volunteer at Voice of Calvary, was driving some Tougaloo College students back to their campus in the next county. They had just been on a peaceful boycott march in Mendenhall. The highway patrol pulled over the van and arrested Doug and the students on a false charge. They were going to teach these boycotters a lesson! Doug was beaten severely on the way to the jail.

When he got the phone call, Rev. Perkins gathered a few men and drove to the next county to see if they could post bond for Doug and the students. But when they got out of the car in Brandon, they were promptly thrown in jail. And then the kicking and beating began. . . .

Several deputy sheriffs and highway patrol officers went to work on the "troublemakers." John and his friends were slapped, punched, stomped on, and kicked in the head, ribs, and groin. Though his face was bloody and his eyes almost swollen shut, John could see the faces of the officers, twisted with rage and hate.

But for some reason, John couldn't hate them back. He didn't want hate to do to him what it had done to them—make them vicious, angry, and capable of any kind of cruelty and injustice.

It was a long time before John Perkins could see a police officer and not feel fear and bitterness. But in time he was able to forgive them because he understood that racism hurts everyone.

Racism hurt black folks because they were treated with disrespect and denied the same rights as white folks. But the sickness of racism hurt white people, too—even churchgoing Christians—

by making them believe they were better than black people. Racism made it seem okay to treat blacks unfairly, even violently.

No, John realized, hating back wasn't the answer. Only the love of Jesus could change people's hearts. Jesus told His disciples to "love your enemies." Even on the cross, while being tortured to death, Jesus said, "Father, forgive them, for they do not know what they are doing."

Forgiveness is one way we can love our enemies.

FROM GOD'S WORD:
Jesus said, "Father, forgive them, because they don't know what they are doing" (Luke 23:34a).

LET'S TALK ABOUT IT:
1. Why did John Perkins think a boycott might be a good way to speak out against the way blacks were treated in his town?
2. What was John's reaction when he was beaten in jail, even though he hadn't broken any laws?
3. If Jesus could forgive His enemies, is there someone Jesus wants you to forgive?

RECONCILIATION
Black and White Together

~~~~~~

Rev. Perkins?" said the caller. "This is Community Legal Services here in Jackson. We're wondering if you could help us."

It was the summer of 1975. John Perkins and his wife, Vera Mae, had just moved the Voice of Calvary headquarters to Jackson, Mississippi, the year before. The work in Mendenhall—which included a church, a health clinic, and a housing co-op, among other things—had been passed on to other community leaders. But the work in Jackson was still very small. John wondered what the caller wanted.

"There's an older couple—a man and his wife—who've been living in an abandoned bread truck outside of town," the caller continued. "We're trying to find them better housing, but we need someplace to shelter them for about two weeks. Can you help?"

John scratched his head. Voice of Calvary wasn't set up for emergency housing, but . . . hadn't God called them to help the poor in Mississippi? "Send 'em over," John said. "We'll see what we can do."

When the homeless couple arrived, the staff of VOC had a

surprise: The man and woman were white! Of course, John and Vera Mae knew there were poor white people in Mississippi, but because of their painful experiences with racist whites, they had largely avoided them. It was easier to minister to their own people.

As VOC staff helped rustle up emergency food, clothing, and a place to stay, John thought, *Well, Lord, you've brought me a long way since 1970 in the Brandon jail. I think you've been trying to show me for a long time that I must not only forgive my enemies and love my enemies, but that you want me to be* reconciled *and live in peace with my enemies. Black and white Christians need to work together and help each other in a* visible *way everyone can see. That is what will really show the world the power of the Gospel.*

But John knew the road to reconciliation would be long and hard. Whites who realized that racism was wrong often felt crippled by guilt. Blacks, in turn, found it easy to blame whites for all their troubles. If racial healing was to ever happen among Christians in America, they would need to get beyond *guilt* and *blame.*

For true reconciliation to happen, John knew that blacks and whites needed to respect each other as equals and partners. This would mean living near each other, working together, listening to one another, asking forgiveness and forgiving each other, and . . . worshiping together.

When Voice of Calvary Ministries established a church in Jackson, they chose to hire Phil Reed, a white pastor, and Romas McLain, a black pastor, to pastor the congregation together. Even though McLain was called to another ministry a short while later, the church remains a "cross-cultural" church, committed to bringing blacks and whites together in God's peace.

For many years the Perkinses also took their message of reconciliation and community development to California. But now John and Vera Mae Perkins are back in Mississippi—although not to retire. They're still following God's call to work for justice in the black community and to bring healing between black and white Christians.

Reconciliation breaks down the barriers
between people.

FROM GOD'S WORD:
It was also Christ's purpose to end the hatred between the two groups, to make them into one body, and to bring them back to God. Christ did all this with his death on the cross (Ephesians 2:16).

LET'S TALK ABOUT IT:
1. Why did John Perkins realize it was important for black and white Christians to work and worship together?
2. In what way are blacks and whites today like the Jews and Gentiles in New Testament times?
3. How could you get to know someone better in your school, neighborhood, or work who is of another race or culture?

AMANDA SMITH

American Evangelist
to the World

Amanda Berry was born into slavery in Maryland in 1837. Her father, Samuel Berry, managed to buy his freedom, as well as that of his wife and children. Praising God for deliverance, the family moved to Pennsylvania, a free state, where their home became a station on the Underground Railroad for runaway slaves.

Though raised by strong Christian parents, Amanda had not yet decided to follow Jesus when she married at seventeen. Her husband was a heavy drinker, but the difficult marriage ended when he was killed during the Civil War. Amanda, meanwhile, experienced the "saving grace of Jesus" during a Baptist revival. Now her deepest desire was to share God's good news of salvation.

Amanda then married James Smith, an aspiring preacher, but her hopes for a Christian home were disappointed. James grew less interested in spiritual things and was often away from home. She gave birth to five children during her two marriages, but only one daughter, Maizie, lived past infancy. When James died in 1869, Amanda, only thirty-two, never married again, even though it meant supporting herself and her child by taking in washing and ironing.

Amanda had a beautiful voice and often sang and spoke her message of salvation and "sanctification," or holiness, in both black and white churches and at camp meetings. She faced many barriers because she was not only a "woman preacher," but a "colored" woman preacher. But her spirit was always gracious, not pushing in where she was not wanted. In everything, she tried to be obedient to the leading of the Holy Spirit.

In time, her evangelistic work took her to England, India, Africa, and back to the United States, where she founded the Amanda Smith Orphans Home near Chicago, Illinois. A humble woman of great faith and prayer, Amanda Berry Smith went to be with her Lord in 1915 at the age of seventy-eight.

OBEDIENCE
Going to the Fair

manda Smith walked wearily toward her home at 135 Amity Street in New York. Her back ached from bending over the washtub all day. She would make herself a small supper, spend some quiet time in prayer, and go to bed.

"Oh, Sister Smith! Wait one moment!" Sister Johns, a friend from church, was waving at her. "Are you going to the fair tonight?"

Amanda had forgotten about the fair. Several churches were putting on a fund-raising event. Everyone seemed to enjoy the merry crowds, especially the young people. But Amanda shook her head. "No. I'm very tired tonight."

"Oh." Sister Johns' face fell. "I have two tickets to give away. I was hoping you could use them."

Oh, Lord, Amanda thought. *Are you trying to tell me something?* Amanda never made a decision without asking God what He wanted her to do. "Well," she said reluctantly, "give me the tickets. If God wants me to go to the fair, I'll use them."

As Amanda made her tea and supper, she prayed about the

tickets. In her heart, God was making it clear that He wanted her to go. But why? She didn't know, but if God wanted her to do a thing, it was always for some purpose.

She tucked some tracts about salvation and holiness in her coat pocket and walked back out into the November night. The hall where the fair was being held was brightly lit. The crowds buzzed around Amanda, but she felt alone and useless.

"Lord, help me," she prayed. "Show me what you want me to do."

Standing at the top of the stairs where people were coming into the fair, she saw two young men taking the steps two at a time, laughing and shoving as boys do. One of the boys rarely came to church and made no claim to having faith. "Speak to that young man," the Holy Spirit seemed to say.

"Charlie!" Amanda said as he was about to pass by. "I have a tract I'd like you to read."

The boy stopped. "How do, Mrs. Smith?" he asked politely. He took the tract and shrugged. "I grew up with this stuff all my life, you know. Guess I have time to have a bit of fun before I become a sober-faced deacon." His friend snickered.

Amanda patted him on the arm. "It's not about becoming a deacon, Charlie. It's about your soul's salvation. Read it, son, read it."

"All right, Mrs. Smith, whatever you say!" Charlie laughed and ran off with his friend.

Suddenly, Amanda realized she could go home. That was it. That was why God wanted her to come to the fair. To give a tract to Charlie.

Several days later, Amanda was once again heading home carrying a load of wash to do that night. "Sister Smith! Did you hear?" a voice called. It was Sister Johns, hurrying to speak to her.

"Young Charlie was found dead in his bed this morning. Can you imagine? Why, I saw him at the fair not three days ago, healthy as a colt!"

As Sister Johns chattered on, Amanda's heart was both sad and glad. *Oh, Lord,* she prayed, *thank you for giving me the strength to obey you the other night and go to the fair. I don't know whether Charlie responded to the message in the tract or not. I leave that in your hands. My job was to obey.*

Obedience is the willingness to respond to God's still, small voice, even when it goes against our own plans.

FROM GOD'S WORD:
[Jesus] replied, "Blessed rather are those who hear the word of God and obey it" (Luke 11:28, NIV).

LET'S TALK ABOUT IT:
1. Why did Amanda Smith pray about whether to go to the fair, even though her back hurt and her feet were tired?
2. Concerning Charlie, what part was Amanda's job? What part was God's job?
3. Can you think of a time you felt God was asking you to do something, but you didn't feel like doing it? What did you do? What happened?

TRUST
Two Dollars for India

Amanda Smith scooted over on the bench under the big tent to make room for two white ladies dressed in elegant hats and black lace shawls. *What a blessing,* Amanda thought, *that rich and poor, black and white, can come together at camp meeting time to hear such fine preaching for a whole week.* This morning her daughter, Maizie, was at the young people's meeting, but Amanda was eager to hear the missionary woman from India speak.

Amanda's heart ached as the missionary showed the small wooden idols that many people worshiped in India. *How I wish I could tell them the Good News about Jesus!* she thought.

At the end of the meeting, the missionary asked people to give money to help support Bible teachers in India. *I'd give twenty dollars if I could!* thought Amanda. But all she had was two dollars—and that was to buy a new pair of shoes for Maizie.

"Give the two dollars," the Holy Spirit nudged.

"Ho, ho!" the Devil seemed to whisper in her other ear. "Won't you look like a fool in front of these rich ladies giving just two dollars."

Just then the elegant ladies beside Amanda stood up. *Oh, good,* she thought. *They'll be able to give a lot of money, and the missionary won't need my two dollars.* But to her dismay, the women walked out of the tent without giving anything. Several more women got up and left.

"Give the two dollars," the Spirit said again.

"Your child needs shoes," the Devil reminded her. "Your first duty is to your child."

Amanda stood up. Maybe she, too, should just leave like the other women. Instead, she found herself moving toward the missionary speaker. "Will two dollars help bring the Gospel to the people in India?" she asked.

"Of course! God bless you," said the missionary warmly.

Amanda practically floated out of the tent. She knew she'd done the right thing.

But the Devil still scolded her. "Don't you know the Bible says the person who doesn't provide for his own family is worse than a pagan who doesn't worship God?"

Amanda felt a stab of doubt. Had she done the wrong thing after all? But the peace of God continued to fill her heart. "I will just have to trust God for Maizie's shoes," she decided.

After a day of lively meetings, Amanda and Maizie were cutting up some peaches for their supper when a little boy ran up to them. "Grandpa says to come have supper with us in our tent!"

Maizie grinned. "Well, Ma, we better go. Brother Brummel won't let you say no."

Mother and daughter followed the little boy back to his family tent. Two extra plates had been set for the camp-style supper. Brother Brummel's eyes twinkled. "Sit here, Sister Smith!" he said, pointing to a place at the table. All the plates were turned upside down to keep the dust off.

After the prayer, Amanda turned her plate up. There, underneath, were three one-dollar bills—one more than she needed for Maizie's shoes. "Praise the Lord!" she shouted—then laughed. The old Devil sure got himself whipped that time!

Trust is believing God will take care of you even when He asks you to make a sacrifice for Him.

FROM GOD'S WORD:

My God will use his wonderful riches in Christ Jesus to give you everything you need (Philippians 4:19).

LET'S TALK ABOUT IT:

1. Do you think Amanda Smith did the right thing giving two dollars to missions when her daughter needed shoes? Why or why not?
2. How did the Devil try to discourage her?
3. In what ways does your family trust God to give you what you need, and in what ways do you rely on your own resources (money, job, etc.)?

FORGIVENESS
The Best Way to Fight

he special service at the Mayflower Mission in Brooklyn, New York, was over. Amanda Smith stepped down from the plain, wooden platform as a young man pushed through the crowd to speak to her. His handsome face was a dark cloud of gloom.

"Mrs. Smith," he said, clutching his hat, "I was deeply touched by what you said about God wanting us to forgive our enemies." The hat twisted in the man's hands. "I want to forgive my enemy, but . . . I just know it won't work."

Bit by bit, his story tumbled out. Charles Brown and another young man, Will Darcy, had been boyhood friends. When they grew up, they went into business and worked in the same office. Both were members of the Mayflower Mission Church. "But," said Charles, "several years ago, we had a quarrel. We both said harsh, unkind things, and now we haven't spoken to each other in four years. Oh, Mrs. Smith, each day that I see Will and he doesn't speak is an agony! I don't think I can stand it any longer. I'm thinking about leaving the church altogether. My wife begs me not to leave the church, but—"

"Why don't you go speak to him?" Amanda asked gently.

"I'm afraid if I do, he will curse me—and I just couldn't bear it."

"If you decide to do the right thing, God will help you," she encouraged. "Let's pray together right now, and you go talk to him tomorrow. Then tomorrow night, come back here to the mission and tell me what God has done."

The next day, as she got ready for the evening service, Amanda got down on her knees and prayed that this young man could experience the freedom of forgiveness. That evening as she spoke, she scanned the crowd. There sat Charles Brown—and his face was like a sunbeam. Right after the service, he came up to her quickly and said, "Oh, Mrs. Smith, praise the Lord! Everything is all right."

"I told you God would help you," she said. "What happened?"

Again the story tumbled out. All the way to work, Charles prayed he would have the courage to speak. Usually, he was the first to arrive, but that morning, Will was there before him and they were alone. "So I just blurted out, 'Look here, Will, I think it is time you and I were done with this foolishness of ours'—and do you know what he did, Mrs. Smith? He jumped to his feet, grabbed my hand, and with tears in his eyes said, 'I've been wanting to speak to you for a month, but I was afraid you wouldn't speak to me.' Both of us were afraid to be the first one to speak! Quickly, we asked forgiveness and forgave each other—and now we are old friends again."

Amanda's heart nearly burst with joy. If God did nothing else during these special services at the Mayflower Mission, it was worth it to have these two friends living in peace with each other. "You know, Mr. Brown," she said, a twinkle in her eye, "the Devil would rather you settled your quarrel by fighting a duel. But the best way to fight a duel with an enemy is on your knees."

Forgiveness doesn't wait for your enemy to ask to be forgiven, but finds the courage to speak first.

FROM GOD'S WORD:
Get along with each other, and forgive each other. If someone does wrong to you, forgive that person because the Lord forgave you (Colossians 3:13).

LET'S TALK ABOUT IT:
1. Why do you think it was so hard for the young man to speak to his old friend who had become his enemy?
2. What did Amanda Smith mean when she said, "The best way to fight a duel with an enemy is on your knees"?
3. Have you fought with someone lately and now find it hard to speak to that person? Ask God to give you courage to go speak to that person first and ask forgiveness.

CORRIE TEN BOOM

The Watchmaker's Daughter

It was no accident that the ten Boom family hid Jews in their house in Holland during World War II. A deep love for the Word of God and respect for God's chosen people, the Jews, were passed on from great-grandfather Gerrit ten Boom to grandfather Willem ten Boom—then to father Casper ten Boom and his daughter Corrie ten Boom.

Born in 1892, Corrie was the fifth child of Cor and Casper ten Boom. She was a sickly baby, but she soon thrived in the warmth and care of her family. Several widowed and unmarried aunts lived with them off and on in the "Beje" (as they called their tall, narrow house) above Casper's watch repair shop in Haarlem.

Corrie and her older sister Betsie never married, but remained at the "Beje" working in the watch shop, teaching Bible clubs, and taking care of their elderly father. The sisters were in their fifties when the storm clouds of World War II became dark and dangerous. Always helping people, the ten Boom family never questioned their duty to God: they must hide their Jewish friends who were being arrested and sent to death camps.

Then they were betrayed. The entire ten Boom family was arrested for aiding Jews—but the Jews hiding in their attic were never found. Father ten Boom died shortly after his arrest, but Corrie and Betsie were sent to Ravensbruck, a Nazi concentration camp. Of all her family, only Corrie and her brother Willem survived.

When she was finally released, Corrie had a glorious message to tell people: that the light of Jesus could brighten the darkness of any prison, and that God's love and forgiveness were stronger than hate. She took this message to prisons and churches all over the world until her death in 1979.

FAITHFULNESS
Betrayed at the Beje

~~~~~~~~~~~~~~~~~~~~~~~~~~~

The watch repair shop of Casper ten Boom and his family was a popular place. It always seemed to be bustling with people—customers, grandchildren, people dropping in for a chat with the ten Boom family (which included several unmarried aunts) who lived upstairs in the narrow house.

Two of the ten Boom sisters never married and continued to live at the Beje (as the house was called) and help their father with the watch repair business. Everyone in Haarlem knew and respected the ten Boom family, who always did fine watch repair work, never overcharging anyone. They lived by the Word of God and were always ready to give someone a helping hand. In 1943, when the German army rolled into Holland, neighbors and friends often found a comforting word or bit of Scripture at the Beje to ease their fears about what was going to happen to their little country of Holland.

One day, a neighbor came in and pulled Corrie ten Boom into a back room. "My son Hans at the university wouldn't sign a paper pledging allegiance to the German army. I'm afraid they'll arrest him if they find him at our house. Will you let him stay here?"

"Of course!" said Corrie. Helping people was as natural to the ten Booms as breathing.

At first, it was only Hans, but when the Nazis began arresting Jews, the house on the Beje became a hiding place. A small secret room was created behind Corrie's bedroom on the top floor, and all the members of the house practiced what they would do if the soldiers came.

One day, a strange man came into the watch shop and asked for Corrie. He looked worried. "My wife has been arrested for helping to hide Jews," he said anxiously. "I have found a policeman who will help get her released if we give him six hundred guilders. Will you help me?"

"Of course!" said Corrie. She sent urgent word to all her friends who were helping to protect the Jews. Could they collect six hundred guilders as ransom to free this man's wife? When the man returned a few hours later, Corrie handed him the money. "God bless you!" she said.

The next thing she knew, Nazi soldiers were banging at the door. The man had been a spy! The six hundred guilders were proof that the ten Booms were helping Jews. Father quickly gave the signal, and their Jewish friends scurried into hiding. As the soldiers burst in, they arrested Corrie and her family and searched the house for any Jews. But they didn't find any.

Later that day at the police station, the ten Booms read Scripture and prayed together. Yes, they were worried. What would happen to them? But one thing caused their hearts to be glad: Their Jewish friends had not been found! Not for one moment were they sorry they had helped people, even though they knew they were taking a great risk.

Many weeks later when Corrie was in prison, separated from her family, a note was smuggled to her. "All the watches in your closet are safe." Corrie knew what it meant. All the Jews hidden at the Beje had escaped!

Faithfulness is responding in God's way to everything that happens, little or big.

FROM GOD'S WORD:
Whoever is faithful in small matters will be faithful in large ones (Luke 16:10a, TEV).

LET'S TALK ABOUT IT:
1. What were some of the "small ways" Corrie was faithful to God?
2. How did those small ways prepare her to be faithful in bigger things, like hiding the Jews, even though it was very risky?
3. What are some ways you can be God's faithful servant today, even in the little things?

THANKFULNESS
"Thank You, God, for the Fleas"

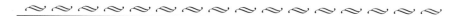

orrie ten Boom and her sister Betsie were roughly pushed into Barracks 28 at Ravensbruck, a "work camp" for prisoners. The two women stared at the stacks of wooden sleeping platforms crowded into the large room. Only a narrow walkway cut between. The platforms were three deep and covered with dirty, stinking straw. There wasn't even enough room to sit up.

They had just arrived by train along with hundreds of other prisoners, crushed together for three days with eighty women in a freight car. Exhausted, the sisters crawled onto the platform that had been assigned to them. But within moments, Corrie sat up quickly and banged her head on the platform above. "Fleas!" she cried, jumping down to the floor. "The place is crawling with fleas! I . . . I don't know how I can cope with living in such a terrible place!"

"Corrie, I think God has already given us the answer," Betsie said. "What was that verse we read from the Bible this morning?"

Corrie pulled out the Bible from the bag that she wore on a

string around her neck. In the dim light, she read from 1 Thessalonians: " 'Be joyful always; pray continually. Give thanks in all circumstances, for this is God's will for you in Christ Jesus' (5:16–18, NIV). Oh, Betsie, that's too hard in a place like this!"

"No, come on, Corrie—let's try. What are we thankful for?"

"Well . . . if we must be in this awful place, I'm thankful that we're together," said Corrie.

"And that the guards didn't find the Bible you had hanging down your back!" added Betsie.

Corrie nodded gratefully. "Maybe we should thank God for how crowded we are in here because that way more women will hear the Word of God when we read it aloud!"

"That's right!" Betsie's eyes danced. "And thank you, God, for the fleas—"

"No, Betsie!" Corrie cried. "I can't thank God for the fleas. There's nothing good about them."

"Well, we'll just have to wait and see," answered Betsie.

Every day, the prisoners were awakened at 4:30 A.M. and forced to stand outside in the cold for roll call. Then they worked an eleven-hour day. They were given black bread for breakfast and a thin soup of turnips for supper. The only thing they had to look forward to was when all the women stumbled back to the barracks at night. Before they went to sleep, Betsie and Corrie would open their smuggled Bible and read God's Word to the other women.

At first, they posted lookouts to keep a watch for the guards. Anyone caught with a Bible would certainly be killed. But day after day passed, and no guards came into Barracks 28. Soon they read the Bible twice a day, and more and more women listened. No one bothered them.

One day, Betsie grabbed Corrie's arm and whispered, "I know

why no one has bothered our Bible studies. I overheard some of the guards talking. None of them wants to come into Barracks 28 *because of the fleas!*"

Corrie wanted to laugh. "All right, Lord," she said. "Thank you for the fleas!"

Thankfulness helps us look for the ways God can use everything—even bad things—for good.

FROM GOD'S WORD:
Give thanks whatever happens. That is what God wants for you in Christ Jesus (1 Thessalonians 5:18).

LET'S TALK ABOUT IT:
1. Why was it important for Corrie and Betsie to look for things they could be thankful for?
2. How did God use the pesky fleas to help them?
3. Is there something unpleasant that you could thank Jesus for today? Try it and see what happens!

FORGIVENESS
"No Fishing Allowed"

~~~~~~

orrie ten Boom looked out over the crowded church in Munich, Germany. The people's faces were pale and sad. World War II was over, but as the raw facts about the Nazi death camps and their plan to kill all the Jews became widely known, the German people seemed shocked into silence.

Corrie could almost hear her sister Betsie whispering in her ear, "Talk to them, Corrie! They need to hear about God's love and forgiveness. They need to know that the light of Christ is stronger than all the powers of darkness."

That's exactly what Corrie was doing. After being released from Ravensbruck, the Nazi death camp for women, she was traveling all over Holland and Germany, telling people that guilt and bitterness would keep them "prisoners" even though the war was over. Only God's love and forgiveness could set them free.

Now her travels had brought her to this large Munich church. After telling them a little bit about her experiences during the war, she said, "Even though our bodies were prisoners in Ravensbruck, our spirits were free. When we confess our sins, God casts them into the deepest ocean." The spry, graying woman grinned. "And even though I cannot find a Scripture for it, I believe God places a sign out there that says, NO FISHING ALLOWED."

Did the people hear the good news? Corrie wasn't sure. When the service was over, they got up quietly and filed out. No one asked her any questions, no one stopped to talk to her . . . except one man wearing a gray overcoat with a brown felt hat in his hands.

Corrie froze when she saw him. She recognized that face. A few years ago, he had been wearing a blue uniform and carrying a short whip, a cruel sneer on his lips. *He had been a Nazi guard at Ravensbruck!*

The man stuck out his hand. "Thank you for that message, Miss ten Boom," he said. "It's good to know that God has buried all my sins at the bottom of the sea."

Corrie was horrified. Did the man expect her to shake his hand? She couldn't! Her dear Betsie was dead—a victim of the cruel treatment she had suffered at the hands of Nazi guards like this one.

"I used to be a guard at Ravensbruck," the man went on. "I did many wrong, cruel things. After the war, I confessed my sins to God, and I know He has forgiven me. But," again the man stuck out his hand, "I would like to know that you forgive me, too, Miss ten Boom. Will you forgive me?"

Corrie just stood there. *I can't!* she cried silently. But as the man stood there, waiting, she realized that God had forgiven her sins. Could she do any less for this man?

Oh, Jesus, help me lift my hand! she prayed silently. Slowly, mechanically, she lifted her hand and put it in his. And as she did so, she began to feel joy flooding down from her heart all the way to her fingertips. "I do forgive you, brother," she said. "With all my heart!"

Forgiveness may be hard, but it is possible because God forgives us.

FROM GOD'S WORD:
"If you forgive others for their sins, your Father in heaven will also forgive you for your sins. But if you don't forgive others, your Father in heaven will not forgive your sins" (Matthew 6:14–15).

LET'S TALK ABOUT IT:
1. Why did Corrie and her sister Betsie believe that God's love and forgiveness were stronger than the powers of darkness?
2. Why was it so hard for Corrie to forgive her former prison guard?
3. What is the hardest thing you've ever had to forgive? According to Matthew 6:15, what happens—or doesn't happen—if we don't forgive?

CAMERON TOWNSEND

Founder of Wycliff Bible Translators

William "Cam" Townsend, born July 9, 1896, was a skinny kid raised on a California farm. When he entered college, he didn't know what he wanted to do with his life. However, the First World War was heating up, and he was pretty sure he'd get drafted, so in 1916 he enlisted in the National Guard.

Then he met Stella Zimmerman, a missionary in Central America. "You cowards!" she scolded. "Going to war where a million other men will go and leaving us women to do the Lord's work alone! You are needed in Central America to sell Bibles to people who walk in darkness."

To Cam's amazement, his National Guard captain agreed, and he was released from duty for a year's service with the Los Angeles Bible House, selling Bibles in Guatemala. It was a year that changed Cam Townsend's life.

Once in Guatemala, Cam realized that not everyone spoke Spanish or could read the Spanish Bibles he was selling. There were hundreds of Indian languages that had never been written down. At the age of twenty-three, he and his new wife, Elvira, settled in a cornstalk house in a Cakchiquel Indian village to teach school and study the language. Twelve years later, Cam's translation of the New Testament in the Cakchiquel language was published.

But there were so many more Indian languages throughout Central and South America! Cam Townsend's vision to put the Scriptures into the Indians' own languages led him to start the Summer Institute of Linguistics (SIL) to train Bible translators. He also began Wycliff Bible Translators to raise funds and promote the work.

In 1944, Elvira Townsend died. A short while later, Cam married a seond time. Together, the Townsends continued to spread the work of Wycliff around the world. Shortly after his death in 1982, the number of Wycliff/SIL workers reached six thousand, working with a thousand different language groups. Cameron Townsend's passion in life—to "translate the Scriptures into every language"—is being carried forward by Wycliff Bible Translators even today.

HUMILITY
"Do You Know Señor Jesús?"

~~~~~~~~~~~~~~~~~~~~~~~~~~~~~~~~

Twenty-one-year-old Cameron Townsend was both excited and nervous as he walked the streets of Antigua, a city nestled in the shadow of the volcano Agua. He had only been in Guatemala a few weeks getting used to the heat and heavy rains, the meals of beans and tortillas, and the rugged trails leading to various towns. But he was eager to get on with his mission assignment—selling Spanish New Testaments and sharing the Gospel.

Today, Mr. Bishop, a veteran missionary, had encouraged Cameron to go out in the streets and do some "personal work" (sharing the Gospel with others). Cameron had very little experience witnessing in English, much less in Spanish, but he was game to try.

A middle-aged man was coming toward him. Cameron's heart started beating very fast. By the time the man was close enough to speak to, Cameron's heart was beating so hard he couldn't get any words out. Frustrated with himself, he turned around and tried to catch up to the man. But as soon as he got close, again he was unable to speak. After passing the man a third time, Cameron gave up.

Oh, Lord, you're going to have to help me here, he begged silently. He remembered being told that asking someone, "Do you know the Lord Jesus?" was a good way to start a conversation. Cameron reviewed his weak Spanish: "Lord" in Spanish is "Señor." "Jesús" is pronounced "Hay-SOOS."

Turning a corner, Cameron saw a young man about his own age. Gathering his courage, he approached the young man and asked, "Do you know Señor Jesús?"

The young Guatemalan shook his head. "I'm sorry. I can't help you," he said politely to the young American. "I am a stranger in town, too, and do not know this man." He gave an apologetic shrug and moved on.

Cameron stood there, dumbfounded. "Jesús" was a common name in Spanish-speaking countries . . . and the word "Señor" was also the word for "Mister." So that was it. The young man thought Cam was asking if he knew how to find a Mr. Jesus living in Antigua!

Embarrassed, Cameron walked back to the mission. Not a very bright beginning, he admitted to himself. But not for a moment did he consider giving up. He would just have to practice his Spanish and learn from the other missionaries. After all, God had called him here, so he knew God would help him learn.

It certainly wasn't the last time Cameron Townsend felt weak and powerless to share the Gospel. Even though his Spanish improved, he realized that many of the Indians he spoke to couldn't speak or understand Spanish, much less read a Spanish New Testament. Many of the native Indians had their own language—not just one, but hundreds of different tribal languages. Instead of getting discouraged, however, Cameron prayed and asked God to help him know how to reach these Indians with the Gospel.

God answered by giving him a Christian Indian friend named Francisco Diaz. "Frisco," as he was called, became Cam's partner, teaching him the Cakchiquel language. Even though Frisco died two years later of malaria, Cameron Townsend was able to translate the New Testament into the Cakchiquel language!

Humility is recognizing your own limits and relying on God's strength to get the job done.

FROM GOD'S WORD:

[The Lord] said to me, "My grace is enough for you. When you are weak, my power is made perfect in you." So I am very happy to brag about my weaknesses. Then Christ's power can live in me (2 Corinthians 12:9).

LET'S TALK ABOUT IT:

1. What were some of Cameron Townsend's limits and weaknesses when he first went to Guatemala?
2. What were some of the ways God overcame these weaknesses?
3. How does admitting our own limitations or weaknesses help us use God's power?

OBEDIENCE
The Gospel in the Beer Garden

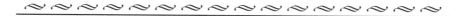

ven though Cam Townsend had been in Guatemala only a few months, a pattern of work was developing. He and a companion would walk from village to village with their supply of free tracts and New Testaments to sell, sharing the Gospel as best they could with anyone they met.

Cam was also watching the people and learning about their ways and customs. He realized that the *Ladinos*—the more educated people of Spanish ancestry—looked down on the native Indians. The Indians were often treated little better than animals, carrying the heavy bundles for the Ladinos, doing their hard work, and getting paid very little.

Cam's heart was drawn to these Indians, especially the Cakchiquel. He figured there were other Spanish-speaking missionaries who could share the Gospel with the Ladinos. He would make it a special point to speak to the Indians in their own language.

One day as Cam and his traveling companion entered the

village of Viega, they saw a Cakchiquel Indian drinking in a beer garden. The two evangelists entered the beer garden and spoke to the man, offering him a Gospel of John. The man shook his head and waved them away. So with a final cheerful word, Cam and his companion left.

They had only gone a few hundred yards down the road when the man came running after them. "My name is Tiburcio," he said in Cakchiquel. "I can't read, but I will find someone who can read it to me."

Encouraged, Cam invited Tiburcio to come to the next Sunday evening meeting held in a nearby village. To Cam's surprise, the man came to the meeting—and when the invitation was given, he stood, saying he wanted to accept Jesus as his Savior.

For many years, Cam prayed for Tiburcio—but only much later did he learn what happened. Tiburcio had been a heavy drinker and was often drunk. But after giving his heart to Jesus, he was never drunk again. His wife was delighted at the changes in her husband—but his friends were not. Why, it was a sign of manhood to get drunk together! But even though they ridiculed and even threatened to harm him, Tiburcio would not give up his new faith.

When Tiburcio began paying off his debts with the money he saved by not drinking, even his employer, the local coffee plantation owner, noticed the difference. Though he could not read or write, Tiburcio was given a job as overseer. The owner could see that this uneducated Indian had become an honest, hard worker. Tiburcio himself never got tired of telling people what Jesus had done for him and his family.

When Cam heard this story, he thought back to the time when he had gone into the beer garden and offered Tiburcio a Gospel of John. "I learned from that experience," he said, "that God could take a poor instrument like me, and if the instrument was willing, He would lead that person into a place of need for [His] honor and glory."

Obedience means reaching out to people who need God, even when we don't know what the results will be.

FROM GOD'S WORD:
Telling the Good News does not give me any reason for bragging. Telling the Good News is my duty—something I must do. And how terrible it will be for me if I do not tell the Good News (1 Corinthians 9:16).

LET'S TALK ABOUT IT:
1. Why might Cam have decided not to go into the beer garden (bar or saloon)?
2. Why did he decide to go into the beer garden?
3. What are some not-so-great places we might have to go if we obey God's command to tell all people the Good News about Jesus?

WISDOM
First Check with the Head Honcho

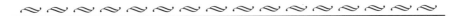

After an hour of fast walking, Cameron and José, his companion on this trip, saw the village of Iztapa tucked into the side of a rugged hill. "There's an Indian believer in this town," José said. "We can rest at his home and get something to eat before beginning our work."

"There sure are a lot of soldiers here," Cam noticed, but he didn't think too much about it. The military had not bothered him before.

After a hearty lunch in the home of the Indian believer, José and Cam started down the first street, handing out tracts to whoever would take them. Cam handed out several tracts to a group of men standing outside a saloon. The owner came out, a middle-aged woman with a wide scarf wrapped around her head and a dirty apron. Cam politely handed her a tract as well.

The saloon owner glanced at the tract. Then with a sneer, she struck a match and burned it. "Out, out!" she screeched at the two men.

Her customers laughed loudly. Cam and José politely said

"Adiós" and decided to try elsewhere. But the townspeople were cool at best, and even hostile. As they tried to talk to another group of men, people on the street gathered. "Devils!" they yelled. "We worship the Virgin Mary!" "Go away or we'll have you arrested."

Cam and José tried to ignore the taunts and sneers, but as the sun began slipping down behind the hills, six soldiers came marching toward them. "Do you have the *boleto de ornato*?" the lieutenant demanded.

Cam did not know what a boleto was, but he heard José say they didn't have it. "Come with me, then," ordered the lieutenant. "You must see the mayor."

The mayor, slightly drunk, also demanded to see the boleto. As José and the mayor talked, Cam realized that a boleto was a receipt showing that each citizen had paid a poll tax. Since José didn't have his, it cost them nine pesos, which included a fine.

But after this was cleared up, Cam told the mayor about their work. "We are your servants," he told the mayor several times. By the time they left the mayor's office, he had listened to the Gospel and accepted several tracts.

"We should have visited him in the first place," Cam said as they hiked back to where they were staying.

Cam was learning by trial and error. He was beginning to put together a way of working. "Observe the experience, discover the principle, and then invest the principle in your life!" In other words, look at your experience, see what works, then use that wisdom to do a better job. For Cam, two important principles were "Observe correct protocol [follow proper customs]" and "Be courteous to people in your host country." Or basically, check in with the "head honcho" or local government first to get their permission and win them over.

As Cameron's ministry grew over the years to include other Central- and South-American countries, following this principle often meant seeking permission from the presidents of those countries. Though some people were upset with him for trying to work with even tough, oppressive governments, Cameron never forgot he was a guest in those countries. He did his best to work in a kind, courteous way so that people could hear the Gospel.

Wisdom is gained by learning from experience.

FROM GOD'S WORD:

Respect for the LORD will teach you wisdom. If you want to be honored, you must be humble (Proverbs 15:33).

LET'S TALK ABOUT IT:

1. Why did Cameron Townsend say, "We should have visited him [the mayor] in the first place"?
2. How do you think Cam's principle of kindness and courtesy helped the work of the Gospel?
3. What is some wisdom you have learned from experience or by "trial and error"?

DAVID ZEISBERGER

Missionary and Friend to Native Americans

David Zeisberger was only five years old in 1726 when his parents escaped Moravia because of religious persecution. They joined a group of other Moravian Brethren who had found safety and refuge on the estate of Count Nicholas von Zinzendorf in Germany. As the Moravian community grew, they sent out missionaries to take the Gospel to oppressed people all over the world.

At age fifteen, David joined his parents, who had traveled to the colony of Georgia in the New World (America). David thrived on pioneer life. He also had a gift for learning languages and had the chance to return to be educated in Europe. But he decided not to go, saying his only desire was to be "truly converted to Christ and to serve Him in this country."

The 1700s were a time of upheaval and change in North America as British and French battled for land and the loyalty of the many Indian tribes, and later, as the Americans fought the

Revolutionary War against Britain to found the United States. But David Zeisberger won the respect of the Indians because he was honest and didn't deceive or cheat them as other whites did. He lived among them, learned their languages, and became their helper and friend. As the Indians became Christians, they formed villages of "Moravian Indians."

The Moravian missionaries and these Christian Indians were both admired for their peaceful, thriving villages, and hated because they refused to take sides between Indians and whites. Twice, David was imprisoned by the British, who thought he must be a French spy. Time and time again, the little bands of Moravian Indians were driven from place to place. They suffered terrible massacres—once at the hands of hostile Indians and once at the hands of angry white settlers.

But the Moravian mission continued, succeeding where other missions failed because they preached only the Gospel of Jesus and did not represent the interests of any earthly country. David Zeisberger died in 1808 at the age of eighty-seven and is buried in Goshen, Ohio.

HONESTY
The Gold Coin

oung David Zeisberger shoved his hands into his jacket pockets and walked quickly, trying to keep warm. Loneliness for his parents, David and Rosina Zeisberger, welled up in his throat. They had emigrated to the "New World" last year when he was fifteen to help build a new colony in Georgia, where oppressed people like themselves—the Moravian Brethren—could find safety and refuge.

But David had been left behind in Holland to finish his education with the Moravian teachers.

Well, it's only a few years, David thought, trying to swallow past the lump in his throat. *Study hard, keep busy—that's the best way to make the time go faster.*

"Say, boy!" a strange voice called out, breaking in to David's thoughts. A tall man in a well-made coat was hailing him. "I'm new to Utrecht," said the man, "and don't know my way around. Could you tell me how to find this address?" He showed David a piece of paper.

"Better still—I'll take you there," offered David. He was glad for something to do. Threading his way through the narrow streets, he took the man where he wanted to go.

"Thank you, young man," said the newcomer, holding out a coin. "Here's a tip for your trouble."

"No, no," David protested. "It was no trouble." Besides, he knew it was against the school rules to take money from anyone.

"I insist," said the man cheerfully, shoving a gold coin in David's hand.

David stared at his hand. A *gold* coin! No one would believe someone had given it to him for a tip. It was too valuable! For a brief moment, he considered not telling anyone . . . but he knew that wasn't honest. He would have to give it to his schoolmaster and tell him where he got it.

But he was right. The schoolmaster did not believe him. "You stole this coin!" he accused. "No stranger would give this much money to a boy."

"But if I stole it, why would I tell you about it?" David asked innocently.

This only made the schoolmaster angry. Grabbing a switch, he whipped David for being a thief.

The whipping hurt for only a little while, but deep inside David was very angry. He had always been taught to be truthful and honest—and to be beaten for it was a terrible wrong.

"I cannot stay here," he decided angrily. "I will run away to the New World and find my parents. They will believe that I did the right thing."

David talked his friend John Michael Schober into running away with him to London. There the boys found General Olgelthorpe, the same man who had founded the colony of Georgia in the New World. With the General's help, David boarded a ship for America—the wild land that would soon become David's new home. In America, his reputation for truthfulness and honesty would be tested again and again.

Honesty is telling the truth, even when other people misunderstand us.

FROM GOD'S WORD:
An honest witness tells the truth, but a dishonest witness tells lies (Proverbs 12:17).

LET'S TALK ABOUT IT:
1. Why did David tell the truth, even though he didn't think the schoolmaster would believe him?
2. What is the difference between doing right and suffering for it, and doing wrong and suffering for it?
3. When is it hard for you to be honest? Why?

FRIENDSHIP
Adopted by the Turtle Clan

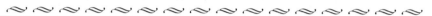

Twenty-four-year-old David looked around curiously at the large circle of bronze-skinned men. All were dressed in their finest shirts, leggings, beads, and feathers. Sixty "sachems," or ruling members, from five Indian nations—Mohawks, Oneidas, Onandagas, Cayugas, and Senecas—had gathered on June 20, 1745, for the Grand Council of the Iroquois Confederation. Two white men sat among them: Bishop Spangenberg, a leader of the Christians known as the Moravian Brethren, and young David Zeisberger.

"Friends," said Bishop Spangenberg, "we have come to ask your permission to begin a mission in the valley of the Wyoming. Years ago, this Council made a covenant of friendship with Count Zinzendorf, our leader, when he visited this country from Germany. Now again we come as friends, seeking to live among you."

The Indian interpreter translated what the bishop said into the common language of the Iroquois tribes.

"Many white men say they come as friends," spoke up one of

the Cayuga sachems. "But their words are not straight. They say one thing and do another."

"Yes!" cried one of the Senecas. "White men trade us rum for our canoes and our land. 'Drink! Drink!' they say. So we drink, and the rum makes us act crazy. Then the whites point their fingers at us and laugh. 'Look at the fools,' they say. But who made us fools?"

There were shouts and nods of agreement around the circle. "Yes! Yes! The whites only want to cheat us out of our land."

A Mohawk sachem stood up. "What you say is true," he said. "But these white men are different. The young one, David, lived among our tribe this past winter. He came to learn our language and promised his friendship to our people. The British in our area wanted him to take an oath of allegiance to their King George—but David would not. So they put him in prison as a spy. Seven weeks in prison—even though he had done no crime! I say he and his bishop are friends, not tools of the British."

One of the Onandagas also stood up. "My brothers, the Moravian bishop I do not know. But I know David Zeisberger. He is more than a friend—he is our brother. We Onandagas have adopted him into our tribe and the clan of the Turtle. His name among us is *Ganousaracherie*."

The sachems murmured excitedly to one another. Indian clans like the Turtle, Bear, and Beaver carried across more than one tribe. A member of the Turtle clan would be considered "one of the family" to other Turtle clan members, whether they were Seneca or Mohawk or Oneida.

With these words, it did not take long for the Grand Council of the Iroquois to say yes to the bishop's request.

As Bishop Spangenberg and David Zeisberger left the Council later that day, the bishop said, "David, I see that your friendship with our Indian brothers has readied the way for the mission we want to build in this valley. You may be young, David, but I believe God has given you a true call to bring the Gospel to the Indians of North America."

Friendship with people different from ourselves can open the way to showing God's love for them.

FROM GOD'S WORD:
Whoever loves pure thoughts and kind words will have even the king as a friend (Proverbs 22:11).

LET'S TALK ABOUT IT:
1. Why did some members of the Grand Council of the Iroquois distrust the Moravian bishop's request?
2. What changed their minds?
3. How can you (and your family) show true friendship to someone different from yourselves or who may not be a Christian?

TRUST

Massacre at Beautiful Spring

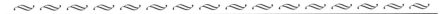

The Delaware chief, Netawetwas, and his friend David Zeisberger were having a serious talk. "Many of my braves want to join the British in fighting against the colonists," said the chief. "They don't want the white settlers to come to the Ohio valley. Three thousand braves are prepared to go to war."

"But Chief Netawetwas, the Delawares are a peaceful people," Zeisberger cried. "Don't get caught in this war between the British and her colonies. Even though Colonel Hamilton at Fort Detroit has been pressuring us and our Christian Indians, we have told him we will not fight."

Chief Netawetwas snorted. "I know. Hamilton, the 'Hair Buyer,' has promised to pay Indians for the scalp of any white settler. But . . . you are right. I will do my best to keep the Delawares out of this war."

Zeisberger watched his friend go. Nine years earlier, the Delaware chief had invited Zeisberger and his band of Christian Indians to live along the Muskingum River in the Ohio valley.

Grateful to escape the drunken fights between white settlers, Indians, and British along the Susquehanna River in Pennsylvania, Zeisberger had accepted the invitation and built a Christian town in the Ohio valley that they called Schoenbrunn, meaning "Beautiful Spring."

But the Revolutionary War had caught up with them in the wilderness. Zeisberger and the other Moravian Brethren refused to take sides—but this caused both the British and the American colonists to be suspicious that the Moravians were helping with the other side.

Danger was not long in coming. On August 10, 1781, a band of three hundred Indians led by a British captain rode into Schoenbrunn. "We have orders to take you missionaries back to Detroit with us," barked Captain Elliot. As David Zeisberger and the other missionaries were roughly taken away, the Indians in war paint tried to talk the Christian Indians into coming away with them. When the Christian Indians refused, they were driven out by force as the war party burned their buildings, stole their belongings, and destroyed their crops.

Driven from their homes before they could bring in their harvest, the four hundred Christian Indians right away built another town along the Sandusky River in Ohio, which they called Captives Town. But as winter set in, they faced possible starvation. Finally, the group decided that ninety people—men, women, and children—would go back to Schoenbrunn and harvest the crops.

Little did they know what awaited them. Months went by, and finally word reached David Zeisberger in Detroit that a band of two hundred white settlers had rounded up the innocent harvesters and clubbed them to death in revenge for the murder of a white settler's family by an unknown Indian war party.

When he heard the terrible news, David cried, "Where shall

we find a retreat, a little spot of earth where we may safely flee with our Indians? The world is not wide enough. From the whites who call themselves 'Christians,' we can hope for no protection. Among the heathen Indians we no longer have any friends. We are outlaws! But the Lord reigns. He will not forsake us."

Trust means putting your confidence in God even when everything is going wrong.

FROM GOD'S WORD:

Some trust in chariots, others in horses, but we trust the LORD our God (Psalm 20:7).

LET'S TALK ABOUT IT:

1. Why do you think David Zeisberger did not want the missionaries and Christian Indians to take sides during the Revolutionary War?
2. Why do you think David Zeisberger was able to say, "But the Lord reigns. He will not forsake us," after hearing about the terrible massacre?
3. What can you do to strengthen your trust in God, even when everything seems to be going wrong?

List of Character Qualities ❧

COURAGE
   The Chance to Escape Not Taken (John Bunyan)
CREATIVITY
   The Jailhouse Preacher (John Bunyan)
DESTINY
   Saved for a Purpose (John Newton)
DISCERNMENT
   Catching the Trickster (Peter Cartwright)
FAITH
   It Rained on Their Parade (Watchman Nee)
FAITHFULNESS
   Betrayed at the Beje (Corrie ten Boom)
FORGIVENESS
   Beaten in the Brandon Jail (John Perkins)
   The Best Way to Fight (Amanda Smith)
   "No Fishing Allowed" (Corrie ten Boom)
FRIENDSHIP
   Adopted by the Turtle Clan (David Zeisberger)
GENEROSITY
   Six Lousy Shirts (Florence Nightingale)
HONESTY
   The Gold Coin (David Zeisberger)
HUMILITY
   "Do You Know Señor Jesús?" (Cameron Townsend)
HUMOR
   The Cornstalk Duel (Peter Cartwright)

DAVE AND NETA JACKSON are a bestselling husband-and-wife writing team who have authored or coauthored many books on marriage and family, the church, and relationships, including the award-winning TRAILBLAZER BOOKS, a unique series of exciting adventure stories that introduce children to inspirational Christian heroes of the past. They have also written the books accompanying the SECRET ADVENTURE video series, the PET PARABLES series, and the CARING PARENT series.

The Jacksons have two married children: Julian, the illustrator for the TRAILBLAZER BOOKS, and Rachel, who has recently blessed Dave and Neta with a granddaughter, Havah Noelle. The Jacksons make their home in Evanston, Illinois, where they are active members of Reba Place Church.